BONIFACIUS: AN ESSAY TO DO GOOD

Bonifacius:

AN ESSAY . . . TO DO GOOD

(1710)

BY

COTTON MATHER

A FACSIMILE REPRODUCTION

WITH AN INTRODUCTION

BY

JOSEPHINE K. PIERCY

GAINESVILLE, FLORIDA

SCHOLARS' FACSIMILES & REPRINTS

1967

SCHOLARS' FACSIMILES & REPRINTS
1605 N.W. 14TH AVENUE
GAINESVILLE, FLORIDA, 32601, U.S.A.

HARRY R. WARFEL, GENERAL EDITOR

L.C. CATALOG CARD NUMBER: 67-18712

MANUFACTURED IN THE U.S.A.

INTRODUCTION

"A good man is one who loves to do Good. . . . If a Good man be in Publick Station, he will be one of a Publick Spirit. Whatever Office he sustains, in the State, or in the Church, he labours while he lives, that he may have that Epitaph upon him, when he Dies, 2 Chron. 24:16. *He has done good in Israel.* . . . A Good Man that may have people under him, will often think, and even with a most Paternal Agony: O my God, what Good, what Good shall I do for my People?"

What manner of man was the author of this *Pourtraiture of a GOOD MAN* and of *Bonifacius*? Did he practice what he literally and continually preached? The truth is that, in spite of some of his objectionable qualities that have clung to his image in our history—his egotism, his sense of his own importance— he was very like the character that he describes in the portrait just quoted.

Doing good was the passion of his whole life, "The apple of his eye." One wonders how popular he was among his school- mates whom he exhorted to paths of righteousness when he was a child. When he was twenty-one, he drew up resolutions of *High Attainments.* Some seven years later, as he explains in his preface in *Bonifacius*, he was impressed by the words of a British envoy to the Duke of Brandenburgh on man's obligation to do good. And twenty years after that, still inspired by the envoy's words, he composed *Bonifacius.* An Essay Upon the Good, that is to be/ Devised and Designed/ by those/ Who De- sire to Answer to the Great End/ of Life, and to DO GOOD/ while they live."

Meanwhile, he was engaged in ceaseless activity in the church, in the community, in the Massachusetts Bay Colony. With his father, Increase, he took part in the decline and fall of Sir Ed- mund Andros, and both were more responsible than anyone else for the choice of Sir William Phipps as governor. Father and son had administrative parts in the affairs of Harvard. Most of all, they preached and prayed and wrote books and pam- phlets. During his life, Cotton issued over four hundred and fifty titles, all calculated to influence the reader for good.

In the midst of writing books, he prayed for their success, but he prayed a great deal more over himself. If one reads his diary only casually, one might conclude that it is one long conversation with God. Thoroughly indoctrinated with Calvin's dogma of election and the necessity of a good Christian to discover his own state of grace (justification), he is alternately abased with doubt and elated with conviction; now lying prostrate on his study floor in the dust, to obtain "fresh Assurances from Him" though he "had been the most loathsome Creature in the World," but at last receiving divine assurance as his "Soul was even swallowed up, in Astonishment of Admirations at this *Free-grace* of Heaven!"

It was the wish and hope of every Puritan to discover his acceptance by God through some mystic answer such as Cotton Mather records in his diary. Free grace alone would make him a part of God's family, not good works, not just doing good. Once certain, however, that he was among the Elect, he was then free—and obligated—to work for the establishment of Christ's Kingdom on earth. The relationship between justification and good works is made quite clear in the preface to *Bonifacius*: "Indeed, no *Good Works* can be done by any man until he be *Justified*. Until a Man be United into Glorious Christ, who is *our Life*, he is a *Dead Man*. And, I pray, what *Good Works* to be expected from Such a Man? They will be *Dead Works*."

In spite of emotional outbursts of doubt and his need for "fresh Assurances," Cotton Mather must have been certain of his acceptance, for the evidence is indisputable that he tried to do good all of his life.

For more than two centuries, his reputation for his activities in the Salem witchcraft trials suffered unjustly, largely because of the malice of Robert Calef, whose *More Wonders of the Invisible World* ridiculed Mather's *Wonders of the Invisible World*, written to justify the prosecution of witches. Posterity has tended to judge Mather by their own and Calef's rational thinking, but Calef was not typical of his age. Cotton Mather in this matter was. With the zeal of a patriot, he hoped to drive Satan out of New England, and there would have been no Puritan who did not wish the Devil's demise, for he and his armies were

constantly at work to destroy their New English Canaan. Even
so, the Mathers were not among those of fanatical zeal in the
prosecution of witches. They were ever fearful that innocent
persons might be condemned, and they persistently urged the
rejection of "spectre evidence," the most potent weapon in the
condemnation of witches. When this testimony was thrown out
of court, largely due to the influence of the Mathers and other
ministers, the whole sorry business came to an end.

One other tremendous effort to do good came eleven years
after the publication of *Bonifacius* and did much to hurt Cotton
Mather's popularity. He put up a brave and determined fight
for inoculation for smallpox. He suffered persecution and an
attempt upon his life. He was no coward.

Less sensationally but earnestly, constantly, and in great
numbers, he wrote and published books and pamphlets that he
hoped would direct men in the paths of righteousness and good
works. And in 1702, he founded a Society for the Suppression
of Disorders, which he wished to be the model for branch societies to function for good in every community. He was interested
and active in such societies to the end of his days. They were,
in effect, in this, our early history, organizations for social service. In his writings and in his activities, he was interested in
the education of slaves, in missionary work among the Indians,
in the progress of peace, in care for the sick and the indigent.

The work of doing good, then, for the Kingdom of Christ on
earth was the goal of Cotton Mather's life. In small matters
affecting his family and parishioners or in large ones that en-
flamed a community, he carried on his duty as he saw it, vigorously, relentlessly, never doubting his calling as a doer of good.
His philosophy permeates his life and his writing.

It is not strange that this guiding light of his life should be
formulated ultimately into a kind of handbook for others on
how to do good. Although the theme was constantly echoed
in other writings, it was not crystalized into one work until he
was nearly fifty. Sometimes a book flowers after years of germ-
ination. Such a book seems to have been *Bonifacius*. As he
nears its writing, the phrases "doing good" and "Good Devices"
become more and more insistent in his diary.

In February, 1709, he records that he "forms and writes"

Devices of Good "in the Morning of each Day in the Week, on the Quaestions for the Day." These were originally jotted down in other notes than his diary—possibly in notebooks or on scraps of paper—but now, as the theme becomes more emphatic, he transfers his summaries for the day into succinct and abbreviated reviews (though not as brief as here given): On the Lord's Day, he asks what "Service is to be done for my Saviour, in the Flock where of I am the Pastor?" Every Munday. . . . what to be done in MY FAMILY," On Tuesday, the double consideration of Christ and his relatives abroad. On Wednesday, "what Service to be done for Christ, and the Interest of His Kingdome, in the Countrey or among other People?" On Thursday, *what Service in and for the Societies?*" (Here he mentions the desirability of more charity schools and more reforming societies.) On Friday, *what particular Objects of Compassion have I to do good unto?*

"Here, I fill'd my *List,* successively, with *afflicted* People. And, I did what I could for them." On Saturday, *"what remains to be done for the Kingdom of God in MY OWN HEART AND LIFE?* I thought,

"That I am favoured with surprising and uncommon Opportunities, to publish many *Books of Piety.*"

In the interest of further brevity in transferring his notes to his diary, for the future he would not repeat the questions for each day, but only the answers. "My Answer to each of them, will be GOOD DEVISED, for which a G.D. will be the Distinction in these Memorials." And so from that time to the end of his diary in 1727, "G.D." introduces each daily recording.

Though the year 1721-22 is far beyond the production of *Bonifacius,* it is of interest to note his pathetic discouragement in doing good after his proposals for smallpox inoculation were not only vigorously opposed but he himself, after he had been reviled and persecuted, seemed completely rejected. Before a meeting of ministers in November, 1721, he quotes again the sentence spoken by the envoy that had impressed him so much, "It has been a Maxim with me, that a Power to do good, not only gives a right into it, but also makes the Doing of it a Duty. . . .

"My Opportunities to do good, which have been the Apple of My Eye, have been strongly struck at. . . .

"I am at length reduced into this Condition, that my Opportunities to do good, (except among a few of my own little Rem-
nant of a Flock,) appear to me almost entirely extinguished, as
to this Countrey. I must employ my Faculties, in projections
to do good in more distant Places. . . at present, *I have done!
I have done!*" Defeated at home, he must begin anew abroad.
His mission was still to do good.

But to return to 1709-1710 and his "G. D." recordings: The
writing of books had been as much a way to influence people
for good as his active work in his parish. The transference of
his notes to his diary and his emphatic use of "G. D." in the
months before the appearance of *Bonifacius* seem to indicate a
growing consciousness in the expression of an idea. In the pages
of the published work, one can discover echoes of his daily resolutions. But the book is much more than echoes; it shows a
development of broad social and humanitarian vision far beyond
his time.

In *Bonifacius*, Cotton Mather exhorts responsible citizens in
various walks of life to do good: in private circumstances, husband and wife, children, relatives, servants, neighbors; in public
circumstances, the minister, the schoolmaster, the ruler or public
office holder, the physician, the lawyer, and many others. He
sees the need for individual endeavours of man to help man and
the need of reforming societies that would be responsible for
carrying out measures to do good. His directions are specific
and often astonishingly familiar to our own times: Of course
the schoolmaster must realize his great calling in attending little
children, and he must teach them the Christian religion. This
would be expected in a Puritan community. But he urges the
schoolmaster "to carry on the *Discipline of the School* with
Rewards, as well as *Punishments*"—the first being preferable.
And he urges that the teacher be gentle with those who are
slow to learn. His advice to the physician, long before our days
of psychiatry, is to consider the patient's mind as well as his
body. "They that have Practised, the *Art of Curing by Expectation,* have made an Experiment of what the *Mind* will do towards the Cure of the *Body.*" And he warns the Physician that
he must be a very learned man and must never cease to read
books. The whole of *Bonifacius* is worth reading not only to

obtain some insight into the late Puritan period but to discover
the mind of one man who was often far ahead of his time in his
sense of social progress and who was moved all his life to do
good.

From his own experience he knows that the task will not be
easy. In his conclusion to the book, he speaks of Satan's evil
and man's inhumanity to man. The Devil may threaten the
doer of good with total ruin. "Yea, and if the *Devil* were Asleep,
there is Malignity Enough, in the Hearts of *Wicked Men* themselves, to render a man that will *Do Good* very distastful and
Uneasy to them." It is a cry echoed again and again in his
diary and in his *Manuductio ad Ministerium.* He knew whereof
he spoke. If the Doer of Good is thus discouraged, what should
he do? "Prostrate in the Dust, you must *offer up your Supplications, with strong Crying and Tears,* to HIM that is *able to save*
your Opportunities from *Death.*"

Cotton Mather's messages to people of responsibility are
plainly and clearly expressed. *Bonifacius* is, in fact, well written.
He was very much aware of prose style as is positively evident
years later when he discusses it in *Manuductio ad Ministerium.*
He could manipulate it appropriately for whatever subject he
chose. (Compare, for instance, his dignified, straight forward
biography of Bradford and his outrageous play upon words in
his short sketch of Partridge, in the *Magnalia.*) The prose of
Bonifacius is earnest, clear, effective, and, as it should be, very
serious. The preface, though serious too, has its lighter mo-
ments. Its style is graceful and relaxed. In it is to be discovered
some of the wit of which his contemporaries speak. Whether
the author was conscious of it or not, the preface fits easily into
the period of eighteenth century essay writing. (The *Tatler*
appeared in 1709-11; *Bonifacius,* 1710). He will comply with
the writing of a preface since that seems to be the custom, although he observes it is often the basis for attack from the
critics. He publishes his book anonymously:

"*Who is* the Author, there is no Need of Enquiring. This
will be unavoidably known in the Vicinity. But his Writing
without a Name, (as well as *not for One,*) will conceal it from
the most of those to whom the Book may come. And the concealment of his Name, he apprehends, may be of some Use to

the Book; for now, "not, *who*, but *what* is the only thing to be Considered."

It was the custom of the periodical essayists to assume the mask of anonymity and for the fictitious authors to be somewhat playful about their identity.

"It was a Vanity in one Author," continues the author of *Bonifacius*, "and there may be too many Guilty of the Like; to demand, *Ubi mea Legis, me Agnosce*. In true unblushing English, *Reader, whatever you do, count the Author Some-body*. But, I Pray, Sir, what are *You*, that Mankind should be at all concerned about you?" Though a little more ponderous, if the whole paragraph is considered, this is not unlike the introductory number of eighteenth-century periodical essays, including those of Benjamin Franklin.

As every student of American literature knows, *Essays to Do Good*, as *Bonifacius* was later known under its author's name, was an inspiration to Benjamin Franklin and the direct stimulus for the *Silence Dogood Papers*. To Samuel Mather, son of Cotton, he wrote, "When I was a boy, I met with a book, entitled *'Essays to do Good'*. . . . it gave me such a turn of thinking, as to have an influence on my conduct through life; for I have always set a greater value on the character of a *doer of good*, than on any other kind of reputation."

The sympathy of Franklin for Cotton Mather's philosophy is noteworthy. Both were humanitarians bent on improving the lot of their fellowmen. To be sure, Franklin was more worldly, lacking the spiritual domination in Mather, but the latter also aimed at practicality. "There is not one *whimsey*, in all my Proposals," he says of his book. "I propose nothing, but what the *Conscience* of every Good Man will say, *It were well, if it could be accomplished*. . . . I will venture to say, the Book is full of *Reasonable* and *Servicable* Things." It evidently was a book of practicable ideas, for it went into several reprints and editions even into the nineteenth century when some dogooders "enlarged and improved it."

In many ways Cotton Mather, the Puritan, was also a man of the eighteenth century and the Age of Franklin. (Read his *Christian Philosopher* and find even anticipations of Deism.) He believed that the best way to serve God was to serve His creature man, and he crystalized practical ideas for humanitarian work in his *Bonifacius*. He might well have deserved the epitaph he bestowed upon John Bailey at his funeral sermon in 1697. He was "A Good Man Making a Good End."

JOSEPHINE K. PIERCY

Bloomington, Indiana
November, 1966

BONIFACIVS.

AN ESSAY
Upon the GOOD, that is to be
Devifed and Defigned,
BY THOSE
Who Defire to Anfwer the Great END
of *Life*, and to DO GOOD
While they *Live.*

A BOOK Offered,

Firft, in General, unto all CHRISTIANS,
in a PERSONAL Capacity, or in
a RELATIVE.

Then more Particularly,
Unto MAGISTRATES, unto MINISTERS,
unto PHYSICIANS, unto LAWYERS,
unto SCHOLEMASTERS, unto Wealthy
GENTLEMEN, unto feveral Sorts of
OFFICERS, unto CHURCHES, and
unto all SOCIETIES of a Religious
Character and Intention. With Humble
PROPOSALS, of Unexceptionable
METHODS, to *Do Good* in the World.

Eph. VI. 18. *Knowing that whhtfoever Good thing any
man does, the fame fhall he receive of the Lord.*

BOSTON in *N. England*: Printed by *B. Green,* for
Samuel Gerrifh at his Shop in Corn Hill. 1710

The Preface.

AMONG the many *Customs* of the World, which 'tis become almoſt *neceſſary* to comply withal, it ſeems, this is One, *That a Book muſt not appear without a Preface.* And this Little Book willingly Submits unto the *Cuſtomary Ceremony.* It comes with a *Preface,* however it ſhall not be one like the Gates of *Mindus.* But there appears a greater Difficulty in a compliance with another uſage ; that of, *An Epiſtle Dedicatory.* *Dedications* are become Such fooliſh and fulſome *Adulations,* that they are now in a manner *Uſeleſß.* Oftentimes all the uſe of them is, to furniſh the Criticks on, *The Manners of the Age,* with matter of Ridicule. The Excellent *Boyl* Employ'd but a juſt Expreſſion, in ſaying ; *Tis almoſt as much out of Faſhion in ſuch Addreſſes,* *to omit giving Praiſes,* [I may ſay, *Unjuſt* ones] *as 'tis to Believe the Praiſes given on ſuch an Occaſion.* Sometimes the Authors themſelves live to *See* their *Own* Miſtakes, and *Own* them. An *Auſtin* makes the Flouriſhes, he had once uſed in a *Dedication,* an Article of his *Retractations* : A *Calvin* does Revoke a *Dedication,* becauſe he finds

A 2   he

he had made it unto an unworthy Perfon. I may add, that at other times, every One fees, what the Authors would be at, and how much they *Write for themfelves* when they Flatter other men. Another courfe muft now be Steered.

If a Book of 𝕰𝖘𝖘𝖆𝖞𝖊𝖘 𝖙𝖔 𝖉𝖔 𝕲𝖔𝖔𝖉, were to be Dedicated unto a Perfon of Quality, it ought to Seek a Patron, who is a true *Man of Honour,* and of uncommon *Goodnefs.* Thy Patron, O BOOK of *Benefits* to the World, fhould be, a General and moft Generous *Benefactor* to Mankind; One, who never counts himfelf fo well *Advanced,* as in *Stouping* to *Do Good,* unto all that may be the *Better* for him; One whofe *Higheft Ambition* is to abound in *Serviceable Condefcenfions :* A Stranger to the *Gain of Oppreffion ;* The common *Refuge* of the Oppreffed, and the Diftreffed ; One who will know nothing that is *Bafe ;* A Lover of all *Good Men,* in all perfwafions ; Able to *Diftinguifh* them, and Loving them without any *Diftinction.* Let him alfo be one, who has nobly Stript himfelf of *Emoluments* and *Advantages,* when they would have Encumbred his Opportunities, to Serve his Nation. Yea, prefume upon one, who has Governed and Adorned the Greateft and Braveft City on the Face of the Earth, and fo much the *Delight* of that City, as well as of the reft of *Mankind,* that fhe fhall never count her Honour or Welfare more confulted, than when he appears for her as a *Reprefentative,* in the moft Illuftrious of all the Affemblies in the

the World : Belov'd by the *Queen of Cities,* the faireft and richeft Lady of the Univerfe.

In One Word, **A Publick Spirit.** Let him THEREFORE, and upon more than all thefe Accounts be, Sir WILLIAM ASHHURST. For as of old the Poet obferved, upon mentioning the Name of *Plutarch,* the *Echo* anfwered *Philofophy* : So now, **A Publick Spirit,** will immediately be the *Echo* and Reply, in the fenfe of All men, and with a Repetition oftner than that at *Pont-Chareton* ; if the Name of Sir WILLIAM ASHHURST, once be mentioned. HE 'tis whom the Confeffion of *All Men* brings into the Catalogue, with *Abraham,* and *Jofeph,* and thofe other Ancient Bleffings, who are thus Excellently defcribed by *Grotius ; Homines demerendis hominibus nati, qui Omnem Beneficij Collocandi Occafionem Ponebant in Lucro.* *America* afar off alfo knows him ; the *American* Colonies, have their Eye upon the Efforts of his *Goodnefs* for them. *Norunt, Et Antipodes.* Nations of Chriftianized *Indians* likewife pray for him, as their GOVERNOUR. To *Him,* the Defign of fuch a Book will be Acceptable ; whatever may be, the Poor and Mean way of treating the *Noble Subject,* which it would infift upon. To *Him* it wifhes that all the Bleffings of thofe who *Devife Good,* may be for ever multiplied.

I will prefume to do fomething, that will carry a Sweet Harmony, with One of the Main Methods to be obferved in Profecuting the Defign of this Book ; which is, For *Brethren to Dwell together in Unity,* and carry on every Good Defign with *United Endeavours.* ---

They will Pardon me, if I take the leave to joyn with him, in the Teftimonies of our Great Efteem, for an Honourable Difpofition to *Love Good Men,* and to *Do Good in the World,* his Excellent Brother-in-Law. The well-known Name of a, JOSEPH THOMPSON, has long been valued, and fhall alwayes be Remembred, in the Country where this Book is Publifhed. God will be Glorified, for the Piety which adorns him, and the *Pure Religion,* which in the midft of the World, and of Temptations from it, keeps him fo *Unfpotted from the World.* It was the Maxim of a Pagan *Afdrubal* in *Livy, Raro fimul hominibus, bona Fortuna, bonaque mens datur. Chriftianity* will, in this Gentleman, give to the World, an happy Experiment, that the Maxim is capable of a confutation. Becaufe a Book of *Effayes to Do Good,* will doubtlefs find its Agreeable Acceptance with One of So *Good a Mind,* and the Treafurer of a Corporation formed on the Intention to do in *America* that Good which is of all the greateft, whereof Sir *William Afhhurft* is the Governour, he alfo has a part in the Humble Tender of it ; and it muft wifh unto Him *all the Bleffings of Goodnefs.*

The BOOK requires that now fome Account be given of it. It was a Paffage, in a Speech of an Envoy from His *Britanick* Majefty, to the
Duke

Duke of *Brandenburgh* Twenty years ago; *A Capacity to Do Good, not only gives a Title to it, but also makes the doing of it a Duty.* Ink were too vile a Liquor to Write that Paſſage. *Letters of Gold* were too Mean, to be the Preſervers of it. Paper of *Amyanthus* would not be Precious and Perennous enough, to perpetuate it.

To be brief, Reader, The *Book* now in thy Hands, is nothing but an Illuſtration, and a Proſecution of that Memorable Sentence. As *Gold* is capable of a Wonderful Dilatation; Experiment has told us, it may be ſo dilated, that the Hundred thouſandth part of a *Grain,* may be viſible without a *Microſcope*: This *Golden Sentence* may be as much Extended; no man can ſay how much. This Book is but a *Beating* upon it. And at the ſame time, 'tis a Commentary on that Inſpired Maxim, Gal. VI. 10. *As we have Opportunity, let us do Good unto all men*: Every 𝕻𝖗𝖔𝖕𝖔𝖘𝖆𝖑 here made upon it hopes to be able to ſay, *When I am tried, I ſhall come forth as Gold.*

I have not been left altogether Uninformed, That all the Rules of *Diſcretion* and *Behaviour,* are embryo'd in that One Word, MODESTY. But it will be no breach of *Modeſty,* to be very *Poſitive* in aſſerting, That the only *Wiſdom* of Man, lies in Converſing with the Great GOD, and His Glorious CHRIST; and in Engaging as many others as we can, to joyn with us in this our Bleſſedneſs; thereby Promoting His *Kingdom* among the Children of Men; and in Stu-

A 4   dying

dying to *Do Good* unto all about us ; to be *Bleffings* in our feveral Relations ; to heal the Diforders, and help the Diftreffes of a Miferable World, as far as ever we can Extend our Influences. It will be no Trefpafs upon the Rules of *Modefty*, with all poffible *Affurance* to affert, That no man begins to be *Wife*, till he come to make this the *Main* Purpofe and Pleafure of his Life ; Yea, that every Man will at fome time or other be fo *Wife* as to own, that every thing without this is but *Folly*, tho' alas, the moft of Men come not unto it, until it be *Too Late.*

Millions of Men, in all Ranks, befides thofe whofe *Dying* Thoughts are collected in, *The Fair Warnings to a carelefs World,* have at length declared their Conviction of it. It will be no *Immodeffy* in me to fay, The Man who is not Satisfyed of the *Wifdom* in making it the Work of his *Life* to *Do Good,* is alwayes to be beheld with the Pity due to an *Ideot*. No *Firft Principles* are more *Peremptorily* to be adhered unto. Or, Do but grant *A Judgment to come,* and my Affertion is prefently victorious.

I will not be *Immodeft,* and yet I will boldly fay, The Man is worfe than a *Pagan,* who will not come into this Notion of things, *Vir Bonus eft Commune Bonum ;* and *Vivit is qui multis eft ufui ;* and *Utilitate Hominum, nil debet effe Homini Antiquius.* None but a *Good Man,* is really a *Living* Man ; And the more *Good* any Man does, the more he really *Lives. All the reft is Death ;*

or

or belongs to it. Yea, you muſt Excuſe me, if
I ſay, The *Mahometan* alſo ſhall condemn the
Man, who comes not into the Principles of this
Book. For I think, it occurs no leſs than Three
Times in the *Alcoran ;* *God Loves thoſe that are in-
clined to do Good.*

For this *way of Living,* if we are fallen into a
Generation, wherein men will cry, [*Sotah!*]
He's a Fool, of him that practiſes it, as the Rabbi's
foretel, 'twil be in the *Generation wherein the Meſ-
ſiah comes ;* yet there will be a *Wiſer* Generation,
and *Wiſdom will be Juſtified of her Children.* A-
mong the Jews, there has been an *Ezra,* whoſe
Head they called, *The Throne of Wiſdom :* Among
the *Greeks* there has been a *Democritus,* who was
called Σοφια, in the Abſtract ; The Later Ages
knew a *Gildas,* who wore the Sirname of, *Sa-
piens ;* But it is the man whoſe *Temper* & *Intent*
it is, *To Do Good,* that is the Truly *Wiſe man* after all. And indeed had a man, the Hands of a
Briareus, they would all be too few to *Do Good ;*
He might find occaſions to call for more than
all of them. The Engliſh Nation once had a
Sect of men called, *Bon-hommes,* or, *Good men.*
The Ambition of this Book, is to Revive and
Enlarge a *Sect* that may claim that Name ; yea,
to Sollicit, that it may Extend beyond the Bounds
of a *Sect,* by the coming of *all men* into it.

Of all the *Trees in the Garden of God,* which is
there, that Envies not the *Palm-tree,* out of which
alone *Plutarch* tells us, the *Babylonians* fetch'd
more

more than Three Hundred Commodities ? Or the *Coco-tree*, so Beneficial to Man, that a Vessel may be built, and rigg'd, and fraighted and Victualled from that alone ?   To *Plant* such *Trees of Righteousness*, and *Prune* them, is the Hope of the Book now before us.

The Men who *Devise Good*, will now give me leave to mind them of Some things, by which they may be a little Fortified for their Grand Intention ; For, Sirs, you are to pass between *Bozez* (or, Dirty,) and *Seneh*, (or Thorny) and Encounter an Host of things worse than *Philistines*, in your undertaking.

𝔐𝔦𝔰𝔠𝔬𝔫𝔰𝔱𝔯𝔲𝔠𝔱𝔦𝔬𝔫 is One thing against which you will do well to furnish your selves with the Armour both of *Prudence* and of *Patience* ; *Prudence* for the preventing of it, *Patience* for the enduring of it.   You will unavoidably be put upon the Doing of many *Good Things*, which other People will see but *at a Distance*, and be unacquainted with the *Motives* and *Methods* of your doing them ; yea, they may imagine their own *Purposes* crossed, or clogged in what you do; and this will expose you to their censures.   Yet more particularly ; In your *Essayes to Do Good*, you may happen to be concerned with Persons, whose *Power* is greater than their *Vertue*.   It may be *Needful* as well as *Lawful*, for you, to mollify them, with Acknowledgments of those things in them which may render them *Honourable* or *Considerable*, and forbear to take Notice at the

pre-

prefent, of what may be *Culpable*. In this, you may aim at nothing under Heaven, but only, that you may be the more Able to *Do Good* unto *them* ; or by *Them* to *Do Good* unto others. And yet, if you are not very wary, this your *Civility* may prove your *Difadvantage* : Efpecially, if you find your felves obliged, either to change your *Opinion* of the Perfons, or to tax any *Mif-carriage* in them. The Injuftice of the Cenfures upon you, may be much, as if *Paul* rebuking *Felix* for his *Unrighteoufnefs* and *Unchaftity*, fhould have been twitted with it, as an *Inconftancy*, and *Inconfiftency*, in that very lately he had comple-mented this very *Felix*, and faid, He was very glad he had One of fuch Abilities and Accompli-fhments to be concerned withal, and one fo well acquainted with the affairs of his Nation. But you muft not be *Uneafy*, if you fhould be thus unjuftly dealt withal. *Jerom* had written highly, of *Origen*, as a Man of bright Endow-ments ; Anon he wrote as hardly againft fome things that *Origen* was (it may be, wrongfully) accufed of. They cried out upon *Jerom* for his *Levity*, yea, *Falfity*. He defpifed the calumny, and reply'd ; *I did once commend, what I thought was Great in him ; and now condemn what I find to be Evil in him.* I Pray, where's the contradicti-on ! I Say, Be cautious ; But I fay again, Be not *Uneafy*.

What I add unto it, is ; That you muft be above all 𝕯𝖎𝖘𝖈𝖔𝖚𝖗𝖆𝖌𝖊𝖒𝖊𝖓𝖙𝖘. Look for
them,

them, and with a magnanimous *Courage* over-look them.

Some have Obferved, That the moft *Concealed*, and yet the moft *Violent*, of all our *Paffions*, ufu-ally is that of 𝔍𝔬𝔩𝔢𝔫𝔢𝔰𝔰. It layes *Adamantine Chains* of Death and of Darknefs upon us. It holds in *Chains* that cannot be fhaken off, all our other, tho' never fo Impetuous Inclinations. That no more *Hurt* is done in the World, is very much owing to a Sort of *Scorbutick* and *Sponta-neous* Laffitude on the Minds of men, as well as that no more *Good* is done. A *Pharaoh* will do us no wrong if he tell us, *Ye are Idle, ye are I-dle.* We have ufually more *Strength* to *Do Good*, than we have *Will* to lay it out. Sirs, *Be up, and be Doing*! Tis too foon yet fure for an *Hic Situs eft.*

If you meet with vile 𝔍𝔫𝔤𝔯𝔞𝔱𝔦𝔱𝔲𝔡𝔢, from thofe whom you have laid under the moft *Weighty Obligations*; Don't wonder at it. Such a *Turpitude* is the Nature of man funk into, that men had rather bear any *Weight* than that of *Obligations*. They will own fmall ones; but return wonderful Hatred and Malice for fuch as are Extraordinary. They will render it a *Dan-gerous* Thing, to be very *Charitable* and *Beneficent*. *Communities* will do it as well as *Individuals*. *Excefs* of *Defert* at length turns into a kind of *De-merit*. Men will fooner Forgive Great *Injuries*, than Great *Services*. He that built a Matchlefs Caftle for the *Poles*, for his *Reward*, had his *Eyes put out*, that he might not build fuch another.

Such

Such Things are enough to make one *Sick of the World*; but, my Friend, they fhould not make thee *Sick* of *Effayes to do Good in the World*. A *Conformity* to thy Saviour, and a *Communion* with Him, Let that carry thee through all !

T'will be impoffible to Avoid **Envy**. For a *Right Work*, and for a *Good* one, and efpecially, if a man do *Many* Such, he fhall be *Envied of his Neighbour*. Tis incredible, the Force that the *Pride* of men, has to produce *Detraction* ! *Pride*, working in a fort of *Impatience*, that any man fhould be, or do more than they. The Minds of men, as One fays, *have got the Vapours* ; *A Sweet Report of any one throwes them into Convulfions and Agonies ; a Foul one refrefhes 'em.* You muft bear all the *Outrage* of it ; and there is but one fort of *Revenge* to be allow'd you. One fayes, *There is not any Revenge more Heroick, than that which torments Envy by doing of Good.*

It is a Surprizing Paffage, which a late *French* Author has given us; ' That a man *of Good Me-* ' *rit*, is a Kind of *Publick Enemy.* And that by ' *Engroffing* a great many Applaufes, which would ' ferve to gratify a great many others, he can- ' not but be *Envied* ; And that men do natu- ' rally *hate*, what they *Efteem* very much, but ' cannot *Love*. But, my Readers, Let us not be Surprized at it. You have Read, who Suffered the *Oftracifms* at *Athens* ; and what a pretty Reafon the Country Fellow had, why he gave his Voice, for the Banifhing of *Ariftides* ; [Becaufe he

he was every where always called, *The Just* :
and for what Reason the *Ephori* laid a mulct
upon *Agesilaus* ; [Because he did above other
men possess the Hearts of the *Lacedæmonians*.]
You have Read, the Reason why the *Ephesians*
Expelled the best of their Citizens ; [*Nemo de
nobis unus Excellat* ; *sed si quis Extiterit, alio in Loco,
et apud alios sit* :] If any will Out-do their
Neighbours, let 'em find Another Place to do it.
You have Read, That he who conquered *Ha-
nibal*, saw it necessary to Retire from *Rome*, that
the Merit of others might have more Notice
taken of it. My Authors tell me, *At all times,
nothing has been more dangerous among men than too
shining a Merit*. But, my Readers, The Terror
of this *Envy* must not intimidate you. I must
press you, to *Do Good*, and be so far from *Affrighted*
at, that you shall rather be generously *Delighted*
in, the most Envious *Deplumations*.

I wish I may prove a *False Prophet*, when I
foretel you one *Discouragement* more, which
you will have to conflict withal. 𝔇𝔢𝔯𝔦𝔰𝔦𝔬𝔫
is what I mean. And, Let not my *Prediction*
be *Derided*, I pray. It was long since noted,
*Ridiculum Acri Fortius et melius magnas plerumque
secat res*. It is a thing of late Started, that the
way of *Banter*, and *Scoffing*, and *Ridicule*, or, the
Bart'lemew-Fair Method, as they please to call it ;
is a more Effectual way to discourage all *Goodness*, and put it out of countenance, than *Fire*
and *Faggot*. No *Cruelties* are so Insupportable
to

to Humanity, as *Cruel Mockings.* It is extremely probable, that the *Devil* being somewhat *Chained* up in several Places, from the other wayes of *Persecution,* will more than ever apply himself to *this.* *Essayes to Do Good,* shall be Derided, with all the *Art* and *Wit,* that he can inspire into his *Janizaries* : [a *Yani-cheer,* or, *A New Order,* the Grand Segniour of Hell has Instituted.] Exquisite *Profaneness* and *Buffooury* shall try their skill to Laugh People out of them. The Men who abound in them, shall be Exposed on the *Stage ;* *Libels,* and *Lampoons,* and *Satyrs,* the moist poinant that ever were invented, shall be darted at them ; and *Pamphlets* full of Lying Stories, be Scattered, with a design to make them *Ridiculeus.* *Hic se aperit Diabolus !* The *Devil* will try, whether the *Fear of being Laugh'd at,* will not Cool and Scare, a *Zeal to Do Good,* out of the World. -- *Sed tu contra audentior ito.* Sirs, *Despise the Shame,* whatever *Contradiction of Sinners* you meet withal ; you know, what Example did so before you. *Quit you like men, Be Strong ;* you know who gives you the Direction. Say with Resolution, *The Proud have had me greatly in Derision, yet have not I declined to do as much Good as I could .* If you should arrive to a Share in such Suffering s, I will humbly *Shew you mine Opinion,* about the best conduct under them ; Tis, *Neglect,* and *Contempt.* I have a whole University on my side. The University of *Helmstadt* upon a late Abuse offered unto it, had this noble Passage in a Declaration

claration ; *Vifum fuit, non alio Remedio, quam Ge-nerofo Silentio, et pio contemptu, utendum nobis effe.* Go on to *Do Good* ; and *Go Well, Comely in your Going*, like the Noble Creature, which *turneth not away for any.* A Life Spent in Induftrious *Effayes to Do Good*, will be your Powerful, and Perpetual Vindication. T'wil give you fuch a *well-eftablifhed intereft* in the Minds where *Con-fcience* is advifed withal, that a few Squibbing, Silly, impotent Allatrations, will never be able to Extinguifh it. If they go to Ridicule you in their Printed Excurfions, your Name will be fo *Oyl'd*, no Ink will Stick upon it. I remember, *Valerianus Magnus* being abufed by a *Jefuite*, who had Laboured (by a *Modeft enquiry*, you may be fure !) to make him Ridiculous, made no other Defence, but only on every Stroke adjoyned, *Mentiris Impudentiffime.* It is a moft *Impudent Lye!* Sir. And fuch an Anfwer might very truly be given, to every Line of fome Stories that I have feen elfe where *brewed* by another, who is *no Jefuite.* But even *fo much Anfwer* to their *Folly*, is *too much Notice* of it. It is well obferved, *The Contempt of fuch Difcourfes difcredits them, and takes away the Pleafure from thofe that make them.* And it is another Obfervation, *That when they of whom we have heard very ill, yet are found by us upon Trial to be very Good, we naturally conclude, they have a Merit that is Troublefome to fome other People.* The Rule than is, *Be* very *Good*, yea, *Do* very much *Good;* and caft a Generous *Difdain* upon *Con-*
tumelies ;

tumelies; the *Great Remedy* againſt them. If you
want a Pattern I can give you an Imperial one;
It was a *Veſpaſian,* who when one ſpoke ill of him,
ſaid, *Ego, cum nihil faciam dignum propter quod con-*
tumelia afficiar, mendacia nihil curo. And I am
deceived, if it be not an Eaſy thing to be as
Honeſt a Man as a *Veſpaſian!*

Sirs, An Unfainting Reſolution to *Do Good,*
and an *Unwearied well-doing,* is the Thing, that is
now urged upon you. And may this Little
Book now be ſo Happy, as herein to do the part
of a *Monitor,* unto the Readers of it.

I don't find that I have ſpent ſo many Weeks
in Compoſing the Book, as *Deſcartes,* tho' a Profound *Geometrician,* declares he ſpent in Studying the Solution of one *Geometrical Queſtion.*
Yet the Compoſure is grown beyond what I deſired it ſhould have done ; and there is not one
Propoſal in it, but what well Purſued, would
yield the mind a more Solid and Laſting Satisfaction, than the Solution of all the *Problems* in
Euclid, or in *Pappus.* Tis a Vanity in Writers, to
Complement the Readers, with a, *Sorry 'tis no*
better. Inſtead of *that,* I freely tell my Readers,
I have Written what is not unworthy of their Peruſal.
If I did not Think ſo, truly, I would not Pub-
liſh it. For no man Living has demanded it of
me ; 'tis not Publiſhed, *To gratify the Importunity*
of Friends, as your Authors uſe to trifle ; but it
is to *Uſe an Importunity with others,* in a Point, on
which I thought they wanted it. And I will

B

ven-

venture to fay, There is not one *Whimfey* in all my *Propofals.* I propofe nothing, but what the *Confcience* of every Good Man will fay, *It were well, if it could be accomplifhed.* That Writer was in the Right of it, who fays, *I can't underftand, how any honeft Man can Print a Book, and yet profefs, that he thinks none will be the Wifer or Better for the Reading of it.* Indeed, I own that my Subject is worthy to be much *Better* Handled, and my manner of Handling it is not fuch that I dare do as the famous Painter *Titian* did on his Pieces, write my Name, with a double, *Fecit, Fecit,* as much as to fay, *Very well done :* and I muft have utterly Supprefled it, if I had been of the fame Humour, with *Cimabus* another famous Painter, who, if himfelf or any other Spyed the leaft Fault in his Pieces, would utterly deface them and deftroy them, tho' he had beftow'd a Twelve-months pains upon them. Yet I will venture to fay, The Book is full of *Reafonable* and *Serviceable* Things ; and it would be well for us, if fuch things were hearken'd to; and I have *Done well* to offer them.

Who is the Author, there is no Need of Enquiring. This will be unavoidably known in the Vicinity. But his Writing *without* a Name, (as well as *not for One,*) will conceal it from the moft of thofe to whom the Book may come. And the concealment of his Name, he apprehends, may be of fome Ufe to the Book ; for now, not, *Who,* but, *What,* is the only thing to be Confidered.   It

It was a Vanity in One Author, and there may be too many Guilty of the Like ; To demand, *Ubi mea Legis, me Agnosce.* In true unblushing English, *Reader, whatever you do, count the Author Some-body.* But, I Pray, Sir, what are *You,* that Mankind should be at all concerned about you ? He was almost as great a Man, as any Ecclesiastical Preferments could make him, who yet would not have so much as his Name in his Epitaph ; he would only have, *Hic Jacet, Umbra, Cinis, Nihil.* There shall be no other Name on this Composure ; *Hic Scribit (vel Scripturire Studet et audet) Umbra, Cinis, Nihil.*

However, He is very Strongly perswaded, There is a Day very near at hand, when Books of such a Tendency as this, will be the most welcome Things imaginable, to many Thousands of Readers, and have more than One Edition. Yea, *Great will be the Army of them that Publish them !* M. DCC. XVI. is a coming.

A vast Variety of *New wayes to Do Good* will be litt upon ; *Pathes* which no Fowl of the Best Flight at Noble Designs has yet *known ;* and which the *Vultures* most Piercing Eye has not yet seen, and where the *Lions* of the Strongest Resolution have never passed.

In the mean time, North BRITAIN will be *Distinguish'd,* [Pardon me, if I use the Term, *Gosheniz'd,*] by Irradiations from Heaven upon it, of such a Tendency. There will be found a Set of Excellent Men, in that Reformed and
Re-

Renowned Church of *Scotland*, with whom, the moſt Refined and Extenſive Eſſayes to *Do Good*, will become ſo Natural, that the whole World will fare the Better for them. To Theſe, this BOOK is humbly preſented, by a Great Ad. mirer of the *Good Things* daily doing among them ; as Knowing, That if no where elſe, yet among *them*, it will find ſome Reception ; They will *not be forgetful to Entertain* ſuch a *Stranger* !---

The cenſure of *Writing too much*, (no, tho' he ſhould go as far as *Terentianus Carthaginenſis* tells us *Varro* did,) he counts not worth Anſwering. --- And, I Pray, why not alſo *Preaching too much*! --- But *Eraſmus*, who wrote more, has furniſh'd him with an Anſwer, which is all that ever he intends to give unto it ; *Accuſant quod nimium fecerim ; conſcientia mea me Accuſat, quod minus fecerim, quodque Lentior fuerim.* In plain Ingenuous Engliſh ; The *Cenſure* of others upbraid me, that I have done ſo *much* ; my own *Con ſcience* condemns me that I have done ſo *Little* The Good God forgive my *Slothfulneß* !

ESSAYS

ESSAYS to Do GOOD.

§ 1. SUCH *Glorious Things are Spoken* in the Oracles of our Good God, concerning them who *Devise Good,* that, 𝕬 𝕭𝖔𝖔𝖐 𝖔𝖋 𝕲𝖔𝖔𝖉 𝕯𝖊𝖛𝖎𝖈𝖊𝖘, may very reasonably demand Attention & Acceptance from them that have any Impreffions of the moſt *Reaſonable Religion* upon them. I am *Deviſing* Such a 𝕭𝖔𝖔𝖐; but at the fame time Offering a Sorrowful Demonftration, That if men would Set themſelves to *Deviſe Good,* a world of *Good* might be done, more than there is, in this *Preſent Evil World.* It is very fure, The World has *Need Enough.* There Needs abundance to be done, That the Great GOD and His CHRIST may be more Known and Serv'd in the World ; and that the *Errors* which are *Impediments* to the *Acknowledgments* wherewith men ought to Glorify their Creator and Redeemer, may be Rectified. There needs abundance to be done, That the *Evil Manners* of the World, by which men are *drowned in Perdition,* may be Reformed ; and mankind refcued from the Epidemical Corruption and Slavery which has overwhelmed it. There needs abun-

B 3   dance

dance to be done, That the *Miseries* of the
World may have *Remedies* and *Abatements* provided for them ; and that miserable people
may be Relieved and Comforted. The world
has according to the Computation of Some, a-
bove Seven hundred millions of people now
Living in it. What an ample Field among all
these, to *Do Good* upon ! In a word, *The Kingdom
of God* in the World, Calls for Innumerable *Ser-
vices* from us. To Do SUCH THINGS is to
𝕯𝖔 𝕲𝖔𝖔𝖉. Those men 𝕯𝖊𝖛𝖎𝖘𝖊 𝕲𝖔𝖔𝖉, who
Shape any DEVICES to do Things of Such a
Tendency ; whether the Things be of a *Spiritual*
Importance, or of a *Temporal.* You see, Sirs, the
General matter, appearing as Yet, but as a *Chaos,*
which is to be wrought upon. *Oh ! that the Good
Spirit of God may now fall upon us, and carry on the
Glorious work which lies before us !*

§ 2. T IS to be Supposed, my Readers will
readily grant, That it is an Excel-
lent, a Vertuous, a Laudable Thing to be full of
Devices, to bring about Such *Noble Purposes.* For
any man to Deride, or to Despise my Proposal,
*That we Resolve and Study to Do as much Good
in the World as we can,* would be so black a Character, that I am not willing to make a Supposal of it in any of those with when I am Concerned. Let no man pretend unto the Name
of, *A Christian,* who does not Approve the proposal of, *A Perpetual Endeavour to Do Good in the
                                                World.*

World. What pretenſion can Such a man have to be, *A Follower of the Good One* ? The Primitive *Chriſtians* gladly accepted and improved the Name, when the Pagans by a miſtake Styled them, *Chreſtians* ; Becauſe it Signifyed, *Uſeful Ones.* The *Chriſtians* who have no Ambition to be So, Shall be condemned by the Pagans ; a-mong whom it was a Term of the Higheſt Ho-nour, to be termed, *A Benefaɛtor* ; to have *Done Good*, was accounted *Honourable.* The Philoſopher being asked why Every one deſired ſo much to look upon a Fair Objeɛt! he anſwered, That *it was a Queſtion of a Blind man.* If any man ask, as wanting the Senſe of it, What is it woith the while to *Do Good* in the world! I muſt Say, *It Sounds not like the Queſtion of a Good man.* The Αισησις πνευματικη, as *Origen* calls it, the *Spiritual Taſte* of every Good Man will make him have an unſpeakable *Reliſh* for it.   Yea, Unworthy to be diſcourſed as a *Man*, is he, who is not for, *Doing of Good among Men.* An *Enemy* to the Propoſal, *That mankind, may be the better for us,* deſerves to be Reckoned, little better than, *A Common Enemy of Mankind.* How Cogently do I beſpeak, a Good Reception of what is now deſigned !   I produce not only *Religion,* but e-ven *Humanity* it ſelf, as full of a *Fiery Indignation againſt the Adverſaries of the Deſign.* Excuſe me, Sirs ; I declare, that if I could have my choice, I would never *Eat* or *Drink*, or *Walk*, with ſuch an one, as long as I Live ; or, Look on him as any other than one by whom *Humanity* it felf is Debafed and Blemifhed. A very *Wicked Writer*, has yet found himfelf compell'd by the Force of *Reafon*, to publifh this Confeffion. *To Love the Publick, to Study an Univerfal Good, and to Promote the Intereft of the whole World, as far as is in our Power, is furely the Higheft of Goodnefs, and makes that Temper, which we call Divine.* And, he goes on. *Is the Doing of Good for Glories Sake fo Divine a thing?* [Alas, Too much *Humane*, Sir!] Or, *Is it not a Diviner to Do Good, even where it may be thought Inglorious? Even unto the Ingrateful, and unto thofe who are wholly Infenfible of the Good they receive!* A man muft be far gone in *Wickednefs*, who will open his Mouth, againft fuch *Maxims* and *Actions!* A better Pen has Remark'd it; yea, the man muft be much a Stranger in Hiftory, who has not made the Remark. *To Speak Truth, and to Do Good, were in the Efteem even of the Heathen World, moft God-like Qualities.* God forbid, That in the Efteem of the *Chriftian World*, for thofe Qualities, there fhould be any Abatement!

§ 3. I Won't yet propofe the *Reward* of *Welldoing*, and the glorious Things which the *Mercy* and *Truth* of God will do, for them who *Devife Good*; Becaufe I would have to do with fuch, as will efteem it, a Sufficient *Reward* unto it felf. I will imagine that Generous Ingenuity, in my Readers, which will difpofe them to count themfelves *well-Rewarded* in the Thing

Thing it felf, if God will Accept them to *Do Good* in the World. It is an Invaluable *Honour*, To *Do Good* ; It is an Incomparable *Pleafure.* A Man muft Look upon himfelf as *Dignifyed* and *Gratifyed* by GOD, when an *Opportunity* to *Do Good* is put into his Hands. He muft Embrace it with *Rapture*, as enabling him directly to an-fwer the Great END of his Being. He muft manage it with *Rapturous Delight*, as a moft Sui-table Bufinefs, as a moft Precious Priviledge. He muft *Sing in thofe Wayes of the Lord*, wherein he cannot but find himfelf, while he is *Doing of Good.* As the Saint of Old Sweet-ly Sang, *I was glad, when they faid unto me, Let us go into the Houfe of the Lord.* Thus ought we to be *Glad*, when any *Opportunity* to *Do Good*, is offered unto us. We fhould need no *Arguments*, to make us Entertain the Offer ; but we fhould *Naturally* fly into the Matter, as moft agreeable to the *Divine Nature* whereof we are *made Par-takers.* It fhould *Oblige* us wonderfully ! An Ingot of Gold prefented unto us, not more Ob-liging ! Think, Sirs, *Now I Enjoy what I Am for! Now I Attain what I Wifh for* ! Some Servants of God have been fo Strongly Difpofed this way, that they have cheerfully made a Tender of any *Recompence* that could be defired, (yea, rather than fail, a *Pecuniary* one,) unto any Friend that would *Think* for them, and *Supply* the *Barren-nefs* of their Thoughts, and *Suggeft* unto them a-ny Special and proper *Methods*, wherein they
　　　　　　　　　　　　　　　　　　may

may be *Serviceable.* Certainly, To *Do Good,* is a thing that brings its own *Recompence,* in the Opinion of thofe, who reckon a kind *Information* of a Point wherein they may *Do Good,* worthy to be by them requited with a *Recompence* to the *Informer.* I will only Say; If any of you are Strangers unto fuch a Difpofition as this, to Look upon an *Opportunity* to *Do Good,* as a thing that *Enriches* you, and to Look upon your felves as *Enriched,* and *Favoured* of God, when He does Employ you to *Do Good :* I have done with you. I would pray them, to lay the *Book* afide ; It will difdain to carry on any further Converfation with 'em *!* It handles a Subject on which the Wretches of the Houfe of *Caleb,* will not be converfed withal. It is content with one of Dr. *Stoughtons* Introductions *; It is Enough to me, that I Speak to wife men, whofe Reafon fhall be my Rhetorick, to Chriftians, whofe Confcience fhall be my Eloquence.*

§ 4. THo' the Affertion fly never fo much like a *Chain-Shot* among us, and Rake down all before it, I will again, and again Affert it ; *That we might every One of us do more Good than we do.* And therefore, This is the FIRST PROPOSAL, to be made unto us ; *To be Exceedingly Humbled, that we have done fo Little Good in the World.* I am not *Uncharitable,* in faying ; I know not that *Affembly* of Chriftians upon Earth, which ought not to be a *Bochim,*

in

in this confideration. Oh *!* Tell me, what *Utopia,* I fhall find it in *!* Sirs, Let us begin to bring forth fome *Good Fruit,* by Lamenting our own *Great Unfruitfulnefs.* Verily, *Sins of Omiffion* muft be Confeffed & Bewayled *;* elfe we add unto the Number of them. The moft *Ufeful* Men in the World, have gone out of it, crying to God, *Lord, Let my Sins of Omiffion be Forgiven to me !* Men that have made more than ordinary Confcience about well-Spending of their *Time,* have had their Death-bed made uneafy by this Reflection *; The Lofs of Time now Sits heavy upon me.* Be fure, All *Unregenerate* Perfons, are, as our Bible has told us, *Unprofitable* Perfons. 'Tis not for nothing, that the Comparifon of *Thorns,* and *Briars,* has been ufed, to *Teach* us, what they are. An Unrenewed Sinner, alas, he never did *One Good Work* in all his *Life !* In all his *Life,* did I Say *?* You muft give me that word again *!* He is *Dead* while he *Lives ;* he is *Dead in Sins ;* he has never yet begun to *Live unto God :* and, as is he, fo are *all the Works of his Hands ;* They are *Dead Works.* Ah *!* Wretched *Good-for-nothing.* Wonder, Wonder at the Patience of Heaven, which yet forbears *Cutting-down,* fuch a *Cumberer of the Ground.* The beft, and the firft Advice, to be given unto fuch Perfons, is, *Immediately to do their beft, that they may get out of their woful Unregeneracy.* Let them *Immediately* Acknowledge the *Neceffity* of their Turning to God, but how *Unable* they are to do it, and how *Unworthy* that

that God fhould make them *Able.* *Immediately*
let them lift up their *Cry* unto Sovereign *Grace,*
to *Quicken* them ; and let them then *Try,* whether they cannot with *Quickened* Souls, *Plead* the
Sacrifice and *Righteoufnefs* of a Glorious CHRIST
for their Happy Reconciliation to God ; Serioufly Refolve upon a Life of *Obedience* to God,
and *Serious Religion* ; and Refign themfelves up
unto the *Holy Spirit,* that he may poffefs them,
Inftruct them, Strengthen them, and *for His
Name Sake lead them in the pathes of Holinefs.* There
will no *Good* be done, till this be done. The
very *Firft-born* of all *Devices* to *Do Good,* is in being *Born again,* and in *Devifing Means, that a
Banifhed* Soul may no longer be *Expelled* from the
prefence of God. But you that have been
brought home to God, have Sad caufe, not only
to deplore the *Dark Dayes* of your Unregeneracy, wherein you did none but the *Unfruitful
Works of Darknefs* ; but alfo, that you have done
fo *Little,* fince God has Quickened you and En-
abled you, to *Do,* the Things that fhould be
done. How Little, How Little have you Lived
up, to the Strains of *Gratitude,* which might have
been juftly Expected, fince God has brought you
into His Marvellous Light! The beft of us may
mourn in our Complaint ; *Lord, How Little Good
have I done, to what I might have done* ! Let the
Senfe of this caufe us to *Loathe* and *Judge* ourfelves before the Lord : Let it fill us with Shame,
and Abafe us wonderfully! How can we do
any

any other, than with *David,* even make a Cauldron of our couch, and a Bath of our Tears, when we confider how little *Good* we have done! *Oh! That our Heads were Waters,* becaufe they have been fo *Dry* of all Thoughts to *Do Good!* *Oh! That our Eyes were a Fountain of Tears;* becaufe they have been fo little upon the *Look out* for Objects & Methods to *Do Good* upon ! For the *Pardon* of this *Evil-doing,* Let us Fly to the Great *Sacrifice;* which is our only *Expiation.* Plead the *Blood* of that *Lamb of God,* whofe Univerfal *Ufefulnefs* is One of thofe admirable Properties, for which He has been called, *A Lamb.* The *Pardon* of our *Barrenneß* at *Good Works* being thus obtained, by Faith in that *Blood which cleanfes from all Sin,* that is the way for us to be refcued from a Condemnation to *Perpetual Barrennefs.* The dreadful Sentence of, *Let no Fruit grow on thee for ever !* will be reverfed and prevented, by fuch a *Pardon.* Sirs, A True, Right, Evangelical Proceedure to *Do Good,* muft have this *Repentance* laid in the Foundation of it ! We do not *Handle the Matter Wifely,* if a *Foundation* be not laid thus *Low,* and in the deepeft *Self-Abafement.*

§ 5. HOw full, how full of *Devices* are we, for our own *Secular Advantage!* And how *Expert* in *Devifing* many *Little Things,* to be done for ourfelves ! We apply our Thoughts, with a mighty Affiduity, unto the Old Queftion, *What fhall I Eat & Drink, and wherewithal fhall I*
                                                                        be

be cloathed? It is with a very ftrong Applicat-on of our Thoughts, that we Study, what we fhall do for our felves, in our *Marriages*, in our *Voyages*, in our *Bargains*, and in many, many other concerns, wherein we are Sollicitous to have our condition eafy. We Sollicitoufly *Contrive*, that we may accomplifh *Good Bargains*, and that we may Steer clear of ten thoufand *Inconveniencies*, to which, without fome *Contrivance*, we may ly obnoxious. The *Bufinefs* of our *Perfonal Callings* we carry on with Numberlefs Thoughts, how we may *Do Well*, in what is to be done. To ac-complifh our Temporal *Bufinefs*, in affairs that cannot be Numbred, we *find out Witty Inventions.* But, O Rational, Immortal, Heaven-born SOUL; Are thy wondrous Faculties capable of no Greater Improvements, no better Employments? Why fhould a *Soul* of fuch High Capacities, a *Soul* that may arrive to be clothed in the Bright *Scarlet* of *Angels*, yet *Embrace a Dunghil* ! O let a *Blufh* colouring beyond *Scarlet*, be thy clothing for thy being found fo meanly occupied ! A-las, *In the Multitude of thy Thoughts within thee*, haft thou no Difpofitions to Raife thy Soul, un-to Some thoughts, *What may be done for* GOD, *&* CHRIST, *and for my own* SOUL, *and for the moft Confiderable Interefts?* How many Hundreds of *Thoughts* have we, How to obtain or fecure Some Trifle for our felves; to *One*, How we may Serve the Interefts of the Glorious LORD, and of His People in the World? How can we now

pretend,

prend, that we *Love Him,* or, that a carnal, and a Criminal *Self-Love,* has not the Dominion o-ver us ? I again come in, upon a *Soul* of an Heavenly Extract, and *Smite* it, as the Angel did the Sleeping Prifoner ; *Awake, Shake off thy Shackles, by no longer fettered in a Bafe confinement unto nothing but a Meaner Sort of Bufinefs.* Affume and Affert the Liberty of now and then Think-ing on the *Nobleft Queftion* in the World ; *What Good may I do in the World?* There was a Time, when it was complain'd by no lefs a man, than *Gregory* the Great (the Bifhop of *Rome*) *I am Sunk into the World !* It may be the complaint of a *Soul,* that minds all other things, and rarely calls to mind that *Nobleft Queftion.* Ah *! Star, fall'n from Heav'n,* and choak'd in Duft, Rife and Soar up to fome-thing anfwerable to thy Ori-ginal. Begin a *Courfe of Thoughts,* which when begun, will be like a *Refurrection from the Dead.* They *which dwell in the Duft, Wake and Sing,* and a Little anticipate the *Life* which we are to Live at the *Refurrection of the Dead,* when they Livel-ly fet themfelves to Think ; *How may I be a Blef-fing in the World?* And, *What may I do, that Righ-teoufnefs may more dwell in the World?*

§ 6. HOw much *Hurt* may be done by *One Wicked man ?* Yea, Sometimes *One Wicked man,* of but Small Abilities, becoming an *Indefatigable Tool of the Devil,* may do an Incredi-ble Deal of Mifchief in the World. We have

feen

feen fome Wretched Inftruments of *Curfed Me-mory*, ply the Intention of *Doing Mifchief*, at a Strange rate ; until they have undone a whole Country ; yea, unto the undoing of more than Three Kingdoms, 'Tis a Melancholy confide-ration, which I am now upon : and I may fay, an Aftonifhing One! You will hardly find *One of a Thoufand*, who does near fo much, to Serve God and Chrift, and his own Soul, as you may fee done by Thoufands to Serve the Devil. *An horrible Thing* !

' O my Soul ; Thy *Maker*, and thy *Saviour*, fo wor-
' thy of thy Love, and thy All ! A Lord, whofe infi-
' nite Goodnefs, will follow all that thou doeft for
' Him, with Remunerations, beyond all Apprehenfi-
' onGlorious ! How Little, How Little, is it that thou
' doeft for Him ! At the fame time, look into thy
' Neighbourhood ; See there a monfter of Wickednefs,
' who to his uttermoft will Serve a Devil, that will
' prove a *Deftroyer* unto him, and all whofe *Wages* will
' be *Torments.* He *Studies* how to Serve the *Devil* ; he
' is never weary of his *Drudgery* ; he racks his *Inven-*
' *tion* to go thorough with it. He *Shames* me, he
' *Shames* me wonderfully ! *O my God, I am afhamed,*
' *and blufh to Lift up my Face unto thee, my God.*

There is a man, of whom we read ; *He Devi-feth mifchief upon his Bed, he Sets himfelf in a way that is not Good.* Now, I befeech you, why fhould not we be as *Active*, as *Frequent*, as *Forward*, in *Devifing of Good* ; and as full of *Exquifite Contri-vance* ? Why fhould not we be as *Wife to Do Good*, as any People are *Wife to do Evil* ? I am fure, we have a *better Caufe* ; and there is more of

Reaſon for it. My Friend, Tho' thou art One
that makes but a *Little Figure* in the World, and
a *Brother of Low Degree*, behold, a vaſt Encouragement! A *Little* man may do a great deal of
Hurt. And then, why may not a *Little* man, do
a great deal of *Good*! It is poſſible the *Wiſdom
of a Poor man*, may Start a Propoſal, that may
Save a City, Serve a Nation! A *Single Hair* applied unto a *Flyer*, that has other Wheels depend-
ing on it, may pull up an *Oak*, or pull down an
Houſe.

It is very Obſervable, That when our Lord
JESUS CHRIST, would recommend the *Zeal*,
with which the *Kingdom of Heaven* is to be Served,
He did not mention an Exemple of *Honeſt Wiſdom*; no, but of an Unrighteous and Scandalous
Diſhoneſty, (as of an *Unjuſt Steward*,) for our E-
mulation. The *Wiſdom* of our Lord in this matter, is much to be obſerved. His Deſign is, not
only to repreſent the *Prudence*, but alſo the vaſt
Induſtry, Ingenuity, Reſolution, and *Heroick Effort of Soul*, neceſſary in them, that would Seek
and Serve the Kingdom of Heaven. There is
no where to be found among men, that *Vivacity
of Spirit* in *Lawful* Actions, which there is to be
found in *Unlawful* Ones. The wayes of *Honeſty*
are plain to men, and they require not ſo much
Uneaſineſs in the Minds of men to manage them.
Whereas your *Thieves* and *Cheats*, and men that
follow Courſes of *Diſhoneſty*, take wayes that are
full of Difficulties: the *Turns* and the *Tricks* with

C   which

which they muft be carried thro' them, are innumerable. Hence among fuch Fellowes, you find
the Exercife of the moft Extraordinary *Subtilty.*
There is no fuch Cunning, and Nimble *Application* to be any where elfe met withal. 'Tis
very Emphatical, to fetch from hence the colours
of *Heavenly Wifdom* !   That which I would now
be at, is this ; That we *Do Good* with as much
Application, as any men alive can ufe in *Evil-doing.*
When *Wickednefs proceeds from the wicked,* it is often
done *with both Hands,* and *Greedily.*   Why may
not we proceed in our *Ufefulnefs,* even *with Both
Hands,* and *Greedily* Watching for Opportunities ?
We have no occafion for any *Ill Arts,* that we
may carry on our Defigns to *Do Good.*   God forbid, that we fhould ever imagine the Uniting of
fuch *Inconfiftencies.*   But why cannot we carry on
our *Defigns,* with as much, and as deep, and as
copious *Thought,* as the men of *Ill Arts* ? And
why may not we lay out our Spirits, with as
Tranfporting a Vigour, to Do the Things that
will be *Acceptable* to God, and *Profitable* to Men,
as any Wretches have, when they *Weary themfelves to commit Iniquity* ?   To reprehend certain Ecclefiaftical Drones, who had little Inclination to *Do Good,* Father *Latymer* Employ'd a
coarfe Expreffion of this importance ; *If you
won't Learn of Good Men, for fhame Learn of the
Devil ! He is never Idle. He goes about, feeking
what Hurt he may do !*   Truly, the Indefatigable
Profecution of their Defigns, which we may fee
in

in Some, whom the Holy Word of God has called, *The Children of the Devil,* may Exceedingly
put us to the Blush.　Our *Obligations* to *Do Good*
are infinite : They *Do Evil* against all *Obligations.*　The *Compenſations* made unto them
who *Do Good,* are Encouraging beyond all Expreſſion ; They who *Do Evil,* get nothing to
boaſt of ; but *Evil Purſues the Sinners.* If the
Devil do *Go about,* and People inſpired by him
alſo *Go about, Seeking what Hurt they may do,* Why
do not we *Go about,* and *Seek,* and Think, where
and How to *Do Good?*　Verily, T'were a Character for a *Good Angel,* to do ſo.　O Thou *Child
of God,* and *Lover of all Righteouſneß* ; How canſt
thou find in thy Heart at any time to *Ceaſe* from
doing all the *Good,* that can be done, in the *Right
Wayes of the Lord ?*　Methinks, That *Word of the
Lord,* may be a *Burden* unto us ; If we have any
true *Honour* in us, it will be ſo! *The Children of this
World, are in* [*and, For,*] *their Generation, Wiſer
than the Children of Light.*　Yea, they Purſue the
Works of Darkneß more Livelily, than any of us
Walk in the Light, where-with our Great Saviour
has favour'd us.

§ 7.　TO the Title of 𝕲𝖔𝖔𝖉 𝖂𝖔𝖗𝖐𝖘 there
　　　do belong, thoſe *Eſſayes to Do Good,*
which are now urged for.　To produce them,
the *Firſt* Thing, and indeed the ONE Thing, that
is *Needful,* is, A Glorious work of 𝕲𝖗𝖆𝖈𝖊 on the
Soul, Renewing and Quickening of it, and *Pu-
tifying* of the Sinner, and rendring him *Zealous of*

　　　　　C 2　　　　　　　　*Good*

Good Works: A *Workmanſhip of God* upon us, *Creating* us over again, by JESUS CHRIST, *for Good Works.* And then, there is Needful, what will neceſſarily follow upon ſuch a *Work*: That is, A *Diſpoſition* to *Do Good Works* upon true, Genuine, Generous, and Evangelical *Principles.* Thoſe *Principles* are to be *Stated,* before we can go any further ; when they are *Active,* we ſhall go a great deal further.

It is in the firſt Place, to be taken for granted ; That the *End* for which we do *Good Works,* muſt not be, To afford the Matter of our *Juſtification,* before the Law of the Holy GOD. Indeed, no *Good Works* can be done by any man until he be *Juſtified.* Until a Man be United unto the Glorious CHRIST, who is *our Life,* he is a *Dead Man.* And, I Pray, what *Good Works* to be Expected from Such a Man ? They will all be *Dead Works.* For, *Severed from me ye can do nothing,* Saith our Saviour. The *Juſtification of a* Sinner, *by Faith, Before Good Works, and in Order to them,* is One of thoſe Truths, which may ſay to the Popiſh Innovations, *With us are the Gray-headed, and very Aged Men, much Elder than thy Father.* It was an Old Maxim of the Faithful, *Bona opera Sequuntur Juſtificatum, non præcedunt Juſtificandum.* It is the *Righteouſneſs* of the *Good Works* done by our Saviour and *Surety,* not our own, that *Juſtifies* us before God, and anſwers the Demands of His Law upon us. We do by *Faith* lay hold on thoſe *Good Works* for our *Juſtifying Righteouſneſs*
before

before we arrive to do our own. Tis not our *Faith* it felf, either as doing of *Good Works,* or as being it felf one of them,which Entitles us to the *Juftifying Righteoufneß* of our Saviour. But it is *Faith,*only *As* Renouncing of our ownRighteouf-neß, & Relying on that of our Saviour, provided for the *Chief of Sinners,* by which we are *Juftified.* Sir,All your Attempts at *Good Works* will come to Nothing, till a *Juftifying Faith* in your Saviour, fhall carry you forth unto them. This was the Divinity of the Ancients ; *Jerom* has well Ex-preffed it ; *Sine Chrifto Omnis Virtus eft in Vitio.* Neverthelefs; Firft, You are to Look upon it, as a glorious Truth of the Gofpel,That the *Mo-ral Law* (which prefcribes and requires *Good Works*) muft by every Chriftian Alive be made the *Rule* of his Life. *Do we make void the Law thro' Faith ? God Forbid. Yea, we Eftablish the Law.* The *Rule,* by which we are to *Glorify* God. is given us in the Law of *Good Works,*which we En-joy [I will Exprefs it *fo!*] in the *Ten Command-ments.* It is impoffible for us, to be Releafed from all Obligations to Glorify God by a con-formity to this *Rule* ; Sooner fhall we ceafe to be Creatures. The *Conformity* to that Rule in the *Righteoufneß,* which our Saviour by His Obedi-ence to it, has *brought in,* to *Juftify*us, has for e-ver *Magnified the Law, and made it Honourable.* Tho' our Saviour has furnifhed us, with a per-fect and fpotlefs *Righteoufneß,* when His Obedi-ence to the *Law,* is placed unto our Account ;

Yet it is a *Sin* for us at all to fall ſhort in our own
Obedience to the *Law* : We muſt alwayes Loathe
and Judge our ſelves for the *Sin*: We are not
under the *Law* as a *Covenant of Works*. Our own
Exactneſs in doing of *Good Works*, is not now the
Condition of our *Entring into Life*. *Wo unto us if it
were* ! But ſtill, the *Covenant of Grace* holds us to
it, as our *Duty ;* and if we are in the *Covenant of
Grace*, we ſhall make it our *Study*, to *Do* thoſe *Good
Works* which once were the Terms of our *Entring
into Life*. *Manet Lex tota Pietatis ;* That was the
Divinity in *Tertullians* Dayes ! There muſt be
ſuch an Eſteem for the *Law* of *Good Works* retain-
ed for ever in all the *Juſtifyed :* A *Law* never to
be Abrogated *;* never to be Aboliſhed ! And
then, Secondly, Tho' we are *Juſtified* by a *Precious Faith* in the *Righteouſneſß of God our Saviour*,
yet Good Works are demanded of us, to *Juſtify*
our *Faith ;* to *Demonſtrate*, that it is indeed that
Precious Faith. A *Juſtifying Faith* is a *Jewel*, which
may be *Counterfeited*. But now the *Marks* of a
Faith, which is no Counterfeit, are to be found
in the *Good Works* whereto a Servant of God is
inclined and aſſiſted by his *Faith*. It is by a *Re-
generating Work* of the Holy Spirit, that *Faith* is
wrought in the Souls of the choſen People.
Now the ſame *Work* of God, and of *Grace*, which
does in a *Regeneration* Diſpoſe a man to make his
Flight by *Faith*, unto the *Righteouſneſs* of his only
Saviour, will alſo diſpoſe him to the *Good Works*
of a *Chriſtian Life.* And the Same *Faith* which
goes

goes to the Saviour for a part in His *Righteousness*, will also go to Him, for an Heart and Strength to do the *Good Works*, which are *Ordained, that we should walk in them.* If Our *Faith* be not such a *Faith,* 'tis a *Lifeless* one, and it will not bring to *Life.* A *Workless Faith* is a *Worthless Faith.* My Friend, Suppose thy self Standing before the *Judgment-Seat* of the Glorious LORD. A Needful, a Prudent, Supposal ; it ought to be a very *Frequent* One. The *Judge* demands, *What hast thou to Plead, for a Portion in the Blessedness of the Righteous ?* The Plea must be ;

O my Glorious Judge, Thou hast been my Sacrifice. Oh ! Judge of all the Earth, Give Poor Dust and Ashes Leave to Say, My Righteousness is on the Bench. Surely, In the Lord I have my Righteousness. O my Saviour, I have Received it, I have Secured it, upon thy Gracious offer of it.

The *Judge* proceeds ;

But what hast thou to Plead, That thy Faith should not be Rejected, as the Faith and Hope of the Hypocrite ?

Here the Plea must be ;

Lord, My Faith was thy Work. It was a Faith which disposed me to all the Good Works of thy Holy Religion. My Faith Sanctified me. It carried me to thee, O my Saviour, for Grace to do the Works of Righteousness. It Embraced thee for my Lord as well as for my Saviour. It caused me with Sincerity to Love and Keep thy Commandments ; with assiduity to Serve the Interests of thy Kingdom in the World.

Thus you have *Paul* and *James* Reconciled. Thus you have *Good Works* provided for. The Aphorism of the Physician, is, *Per Brachium fit Judicium de corde.* The *Doings* of Men are truer and surer Indications, than all their *Sayings,* of

C 4

what

what they are *within*. But there is yet a further Confideration, upon which you muft be *Zealoufly Affected* for them. You muft Confider *Good Works,* as the *Way* to, yea, as a *Part* of, the *Great Salvation,* which is Purchafed and Intended for you, by your Bleffed Saviour. Without an *Holy Heart* you can't be fit for an *Holy Heaven ; Meet for the Inheritance of the Holy Ones* in that *Light,* which admits no *works of Darknefs ;* where none but *Good Works* are done for Eternal Ages. But an *Holy Heart* will caufe a man to do *Good works* with all his Heart. The Motto on the Gates of the Holy City is ; 𝔑𝔬𝔫𝔢 𝔟𝔲𝔱 𝔱𝔥𝔢 𝔏𝔬𝔟𝔢𝔯𝔰 𝔬𝔣 𝔊𝔬𝔬𝔡 𝔚𝔬𝔯𝔨𝔰 𝔱𝔬 𝔢𝔫𝔱𝔢𝔯 𝔥𝔢𝔯𝔢. Tis implied, in what we read, *Without Holinefs no man fhall fee the Lord.* Yea, to be *Saved* without *Good works,* were to be *Saved* without *Salvation.* Much of our *Salvation* lies in doing of *Good works.* When our *Souls* are *Enlarged* and *Unfetter'd,* it is that we may *Do* fuch Things. *Heaven* is begun upon *Earth* in the doing of them. Doubtlefs, no man fhall come up to *Heaven,* who is not fo perfwaded. I will mention but one more of thofe *Principles,* which *Good works* grow upon. Tis that Noble one, of GRATITUDE. The Believer cannot but Enquire, *What fhall I render to my Saviour?* The Refult of the Enquiry will be, *with Good works to Glorify Him.* We read, *Faith works by Love.* Our *Faith* will firft fhow us the Matchlefs and Marvellous *Love* of God, in Saving us. And the *Faith* of this *Love* will work upon our
Hearts,

Hearts, until it has raiſed in us, an Unquencha-
ble Flame of *Love* unto Him that hath ſo *Loved*
us, and *Saved* us.

Theſe, Theſe are to be our Diſpoſitions ;

*O my Saviour ; Haſt thou done ſo much for me ? Now will
I do all I can for thy Kingdom, and People in the World?
Oh ! What Service is there that I may now do for my Sa-
viour, and for His People in the World !*

Theſe are the Principles to be proceeded on!
And on them, I will obſerve to you a Notable
Thing. Tis worthy of Obſervation, That there
are no men in the World, who ſo abound in
Good works, as the men who have moſt of all a-
bandoned all pretence to *Merit* by their *works.*
There are *Proteſtants* who have out-done *Papiſts,*
in our Days, as well as in Dr.*Willets.* No *Merit-
Mongers* have gone beyond ſome Holy Chriſtians,
who have done *Good works,* upon the *Aſſurance*
of their being already Juſtified and Entitled unto
Life Eternal.

I take Notice, that our Apoſtle, caſting a Juſt
Contempt on the *Endleſs Genealogies,* and Long,
Intricate, Perplexed Pedigrees, which the *Jews*
of his Time, ſtood ſo much upon ; Propoſes in-
ſtead thereof to be Studied, *Charity, out of a Pure
Heart, and a Good Conſcience, and Faith Unfeigned.*
As if he had ſaid, I will give you a *Genealogy*
worth Ten Thouſand of theirs, Firſt,From *Faith
Unfeigned* proceeds a *Good Conſcience* : From a *Good
Conſcience* proceeds a *Pure Heart* : From a *Pure
Heart* proceeds a *Charity* to all about us. Tis
Admirably Stated !

§ 8.

§ 8. **I**T is to be fear'd, That we too seldom *Enquire* after our 𝔒𝔭𝔭𝔬𝔯𝔱𝔲𝔫𝔦𝔱𝔦𝔢𝔰 𝔱𝔬 𝔇𝔬 𝔊𝔬𝔬𝔡. Our *Opportunities to Do Good* are our TALENTS. An awful Account muſt be rendred unto the Great GOD, concerning our Uſe of the 𝔗𝔞𝔩𝔢𝔫𝔱𝔰, wherewith He has Entruſted us, in theſe Precious *Opportunities.* We do not *Uſe* our *Opportunities*, many times becauſe we do not *Know* what they are; and many times, the Reaſon why we do not *Know*, is be-cauſe we do not *Think.* Our *Opportunities to do Good*, ly by Unregarded, and Un-improved; and ſo 'tis but a mean Account that can be given of them. We *Read* of a thing, which we *Deride* as often as we behold; *There is, that maketh himſelf Poor, and yet has great Riches.* It is a thing too too frequently Exemplified, in our *Opportunities to Do Good*, which are ſome of our moſt Valuable *Riches.* Many a man ſeems to reckon himſelf deſtitute of thoſe *Talents*; as if there were *Nothing* for him to do: He pretends he is not in a Condition to *Do* any *Good. Alas! Poor Man; what can he do?* My Friend; *Think* again; *Think* often. *Enquire* what your *Opportunities* are. You will doubtleſs find them, to be more than you were *Aware* of. *Plain Men dwelling in Tents*, Per-ſons of a very *Ordinary Character*, may in a way of bright Piety, prove Perſons of *Extraordinary Uſefulneſs.* A Poor *John Urich* may make a *Gro-tius* the Better for him. I have read of a Pious

Weaver,

Weaver, of whom fome Eminent Perfons would fay, *Chrift walked as it were alive upon the Earth in that man.* And a world of *Good* was done by that man. A mean *Mechanick,* who can tell what an *Engine* of *Good,* he may be, if humbly and wifely applied unto it!

This then is the Next PROPOSAL. Without abridging your felves of your *Occafional Thoughts* on the Queftion, often every Day, *What Good may I do?* State a *Time* now and then for more *Deliberate Thoughts* upon it. Can't you find a *Time,* [Suppofe, once a Week, yea, and how a-greeably, on the *Lord's* Day,] to take that Queftion into your Confideration ; 𝕮𝖍𝖆𝖙 𝖎𝖘 𝖙𝖍𝖊𝖗𝖊 𝖙𝖍𝖆𝖙 𝕴 𝖒𝖆𝖞 𝖉𝖔, 𝖋𝖔𝖗 𝖙𝖍𝖊 𝕾𝖊𝖗𝖛𝖎𝖈𝖊 𝖔𝖋 𝖙𝖍𝖊 𝕲𝖑𝖔𝖗𝖎𝖔𝖚𝖘 𝕷𝖔𝖗𝖉, 𝖆𝖓𝖉 𝖋𝖔𝖗 𝖙𝖍𝖊 𝕮𝖊𝖑𝖋𝖆𝖗𝖊 𝖔𝖋 𝖙𝖍𝖔𝖘𝖊, 𝖋𝖔𝖗 𝖜𝖍𝖔𝖒 𝕴 𝖔𝖚𝖌𝖍𝖙 𝖙𝖔 𝖇𝖊 𝕮𝖔𝖓𝖈𝖊𝖗𝖓𝖊𝖉? Having implored the *Direction* of God, who is the *Father of Lights,* and the Author and Giver of *Good Thoughts, Confider* on the matter, in the various Afpects of it. *Confider* till you have *Refolved* on fomething. The *Refolutions* which you *take up,* immediately *write down.* Examine what *Precept* and what *Promife,* you can find in the Word of God, that may Countenance the Intentions, in thefe your *Memorials.* Look over the *Memorials* at proper Sea-fons afterwards, to fee how far you have Pro-ceeded in the Execution of them. The Advan-tages of thefe *Referved* and *Revifed* 𝕸𝖊𝖒𝖔𝖗𝖎-𝖆𝖑𝖘, no *Rhetorick* will ferve to Commend them,

no

no *Arithmetick* to Number them. There are some *Animals*, of whom we say, *They do not know their own Strength*. *Christians*, why should you be *They*?

§ 9. **L**ET us descend unto 𝕻𝖆𝖗𝖙𝖎𝖈𝖚𝖑𝖆𝖗𝖘. But in doing so, let it not be imagined, that I pretend unto an Enumeration of all the 𝕲𝖔𝖔𝖉 𝕯𝖊𝖛𝖎𝖈𝖊𝖘, that are to be thought upon. Indeed, not a *Thousandth* part of them, need or can be now Enumerated. The *Essay*, which I am now upon, is, only to dig open the several *Springs* of *Usefulness*; which having once begun to Run, will spread into *Streams*, which no *Humane Foresight* can Comprehend. *Spring up, O Well!* So will every true *Israelite* Sing, upon every 𝕻𝖗𝖔𝖕𝖔𝖘𝖆𝖑 here Exhibited. And the *Nobles of Israel* can do nothing more agreeable to their own Character, than to fall to work upon it. Perhaps almost every *Proposal* to be now mentioned, may be like a *Stone* falling on a *Pool*; *Reader*, Keep thy Mind *Calm*, and see, whether the Effect prove not so! That one *Circle* (and *Service*) will produce another, until they Extend, who can tell, how far? and they cannot be reckoned up. The men who give themselves up to 𝕲𝖔𝖔𝖉 𝕯𝖊𝖛𝖎𝖈𝖊𝖘, and who take a due Notice of their *Opportunities to Do Good*, usually find a strange Growth of their *Opportunities*. The Gracious and Faithful Providence of the Glorious Lord, Grants this Recompence unto His Diligent

Diligent Servants, that He will *Multiply* their *Opportunities* to be *Serviceable.* And when Ingenious men, have a little ufed themfelves unto *Contrivances,* in this or that way of Purfuing the beft Intentions, their Ingenuity will fenfibly improve, and there will be more of *Exquifitenefs,* more of *Expanfion,* in their Diffufive Applications. Among all the Difpenfations of *Special Providence,* in the Government of the World, there is none more *Uninterrupted,* than the Accomplifhment of that Word, **Unto him that hath, fhall be given.** I will fay this ; *O Ufeful Man,* Take that for thy *Motto* ; HABENTI DABITUR : And, in a Lively Ufe of thy *Opportunities to Do Good,* fee how notably, it will be accomplifhed! Sir, See what Accomplifhment of that Word will at laft Surprize you; *Tho' thy Beginning were Small, yet thy Latter End fhall greatly Increafe.*

§ 10. ODI *Sapientem qui fibi non fapit.* The *Charity* we are upon, why fhould it not *Begin at Home* ? It obferves not a due *Decorum,* if it do not fo ; and it will be liable to great Exceptions in its Pretenfions and Proceedings.

This then is to be made as an Early PROPOSAL.

Firft, Let every man *Devife* what *Good* may be done, for the Help of what is yet Amifs, **in his own Heart and Life.** It is a Good Note of the Witty *Fullers ; He need not Complain of too little work, who hath a Little World in himfelf to Mend.*

Mend. It was of old Complained; *No man Repented him, saying, What have I done ?* Every man upon Earth may find in himself something that wants Mending ; and the Work of *Repentance* is to Enquire, not only, *What we have done,* but also, *What we have to do ?* Frequent 𝕾𝖊𝖑𝖋-𝕰𝖝𝖆𝖒𝖎𝖓𝖆𝖙𝖎𝖔𝖓, is the Duty and the Prudence, of all that would *Know themselves,* or would not *Lose themselves.* The Great Intention of 𝕾𝖊𝖑𝖋-𝕰𝖝𝖆𝖒𝖎𝖓𝖆𝖙𝖎𝖔𝖓 is, to find out, the Points, wherein we are to, *Amend our wayes.* A Christian that would thrive in Christianity, must be no Stranger to a Course of 𝕸𝖊𝖉𝖎𝖙𝖆𝖙𝖎𝖔𝖓. *Meditation,* Tis one of the *Masters* to make a *Man of God.* One Article and Exercise in our *Meditation,* should be, to find out, the Things wherein a Greater *Conformity* to the *Truths* upon which we have been Meditating, must be Endeavoured If we would be *Good Men,* we must often *Devise* How we may grow in *Knowledge. and in all Goodness* ! It is an Enquiry often to be made ;

What shall I do, that what is yet Lacking in the Image of God upon me, may be Perfected? What shall I do, that I may Live more Perfectly, more Watchfully, more Fruitfully before the Glorious Lord ?

And why should not our *Meditation,* when we Retire to that *Soul-Enriching* Work of Shaping the *Right Thoughts of the Righteous,* Expire with some *Resolution !* *Devise* now, and *Resolve* something, to strengthen your *Walk with God.*

With some Devout *Hearers* of the Word, it is a
Practice

Practice, when they have Heard a Sermon, to think ; *What Good thing have I now to ask of God, with a special Importunity* ? Yea, they use to call upon their *Children* also, and make them answer this Question : *Child,* What Blessing will you now ask of the Glorious God ? And Charge them then to go, and do accordingly.

In pursuance of this Piety, why may not this be one of the Exercises, that shall go to make with us a *Good Evening for the Best of Days* ? On the *Lords-Day Evening,* we may make this one of our Exercises ; To Employ most serious and awful Thoughts on that Question ; *Should I Dy this Week, what have I left Undone, which I should then wish I had made more speed in the doing of* ? My Friend, Place thy self in *Dying* Circumstances ; Apprehend and Realize thy Approaching *Death.* Suppose thy Last Hour come ; the *Decretory Hour*: thy Breath failing, thy Throat rattling, thy Hands with a cold Sweat upon them, only the turn of the Tide expected for thy Expiration. In this Condition ; *What wouldest thou wish to have done, more than thou hast already done, for thy own Soul, for thy Family, or for the People of God* ? Think ; Don't *Forget* the Result of thy Thoughts ; Don't *Delay* to do what thou hast Resolved upon. How much more Agreeable and Profitable, would such an Exercise be on the *Lords-Day Evening,* than those Vanities whereto that *Evening* is too commonly Prostituted, and all the *Good* of the foregoing *Day* Defeated ? And if such an Exercise

were

were often attended, Oh ! How much would it Regulate our Lives ; how Watchfully, how Fruitfully would it cause us to Live ; What an incredible Number of *Good Works* would it produce in the World ?

Will you Remember, Sirs, Every Christian is, *A Temple of God.* It would be a Service to Christianity, if this Notion of Christianity were more often, and clearly Cultivated. But certainly, there yet remains very much, for every one of us to do, that so the *Temple* may be carried on unto Perfection ; Repaired, Finished, Purified ; and the Top-stone of it Laid, with a Shout of *Grace* ! *Grace* ! unto it.

As a Branch of this Piety, I will recommend, a serious and fruitful Improvement, of the Various *Dispensations*, which the Divine Providence obliges us, to take notice of.

More Particularly ;

Have you received any *special Blessings* and *Mercies,* from the Hand of a Merciful God ? You do not suitably Express your Thankfulness ; You do not *render again according to the Benefit that is done unto you* ; Except you set your self to Consider, *What shall I render to the Lord ?* You should Contrive some *Signal Thing* to be done on this Occasion ; Some *Service* to the Kingdom of God, Either within your self, or among others, that may be a just Confession and Remembrance of what a Good God has done for you. Tis what the *Goodness of God leads* you to ! I beseech
you,

you, Sirs ; How can a *Good Voyage,*yea, or a *Good Bargain* be made, without fome *Special Returns* of *Gratitude* unto God ? I would now, have fome-thing of your *Eftates* made a *Thank-Offering,*in be-ing Set apart for *Pious Ufes.*

Whole *Days of Thanksgiving* are to be kept,when the Favours of God rife to a more obfervable Heighth. Chriftians of theFiner Mould,keep their *Private* ones,their *Secret* ones,as well as bear their part in the *Publick.* One Exercife for fuch a Day, is, To take a *Lift* of the more diftinguifhable Suc-cours,and Bounties,wherewith our God has com-forted us. And then,to contrive Some *Notable Ac-knowledgments* of the Glorious Lord, in Endea-vours to Serve Him, and this by way of *Gratitude* for thefe Undeferved Comforts.

On the other hand. You meet with heavy and grievous *Afflictions.* Verily, Tis Pitty to be at the Trouble of Suffering *Afflictions,* and not *get Good* by them. We *get Good* by them, when they awaken us to *Do Good.* I may fay, Never till then ! When God is *Diftributing Sorrows* unto you, the *Sorrows* come ftill upon fome *Errands* : The beft way for you to find, that they do not come *in His Anger,* is for you to Mind the *Er-rands.* The Advice is, That when any *Affliction* comes upon you, You immediately confider, *What Special Article of Repentance does this Affliction call me to ? What Mifcarriage does this Affliction find in me, to be Repented of ?* And then, while the fenfe of the *Affliction* is yet upon you,Sollicitouf-

D ly

ly Confider, *What Improvement in Godlineß and Ufefulneß does this Affliction call me to?* Be more Sollicitous to Gain this point, than to Get out of your *Affliction.* Oh! the *Peace* that will compofe and Poffefs and Ravifh your Minds, when your *Affliction* fhall be found yielding the *Fruits of Rightcoufneß!*

Luther did well to call Afflictions, *Theologiam Chriftianorum.* This may be a fit Place, to introduce One Direction more. We are Travelling thro' a *Malicious* and *Calumnious,* and *Abufive* World. Why fhould not *Malice* be a *Good Informer?* We may be unjuftly *Defamed;* it will be Strange if we are not Frequently fo. A *Defamation* is commonly Refented as a *Provocation.* My Friend, Make it only a *Provocation to Good Works!* The Thing to be now directed is this. Upon any *Reproach,* inftead of being tranfported into a Rage at *Shimei,* Retire, and Patiently Ponder, *Has not God bidden fuch a Reproach, to awaken me unto fome Duty? Unto what fpecial Inftance or Service of Piety, fhould I be awakened, by the Reproach that is caft upon me!* One thus Expreffes it. *The Backbiters Tongue, like a Mill-clack will be ftill Wagging, that he may Grind thy Good Name to Powder. Learn therefore to make fuch ufe of his Clack as to make thy Bread by it ; I mean, To live fo, that no Credit fhall be given to Slander.* Thus all the *Abufes* you meet withal, may prove unto you in the Hand of a Faithful God, no other than the Strokes which a Statuary Employes on his Ill-Shaped

Shaped Marble ; only to form you into a more
beautiful Shape, and make you fitter to adorn
the Heavenly Temple. Sirs, you are put into,
a way to *ſhake off a Viper*, how advantageouſly !

Yea, I am going to ſhow you, how you may
fetch a Treacle out of a Viper. Auſtin would have
our very *Sins*, come into the Invoyſe of the, *All
Things*, that are to *Work together for Good.* Where-
fore, firſt, I move, That our former *Barrenneß*
may now be Look'd upon, as our Obligation
and Incitation to a Greater *Fruitfulneß.* But
this motion is too general. I will deſcend unto
a notable Particularity. I would look back, upon my paſt Life, and call to Mind what more
Singular Out-breakings of Sin have blemiſhed it,
and been the *Reproach of my Youth.* Now, by way
of *Thankfulneſs* for that *Grace* of God, and that
Blood of His *Chriſt,* thro' which my *Crimes* have
been Pardoned, I would Set my ſelf to think,
*What Vertues, and what Actions, and what Atchieve-
ments for the Kingdom of God, will be the moſt contrary
to my former Blemiſhes ? And what Efforts of Goodneſs, will be the nobleſt and moſt palpable contradiction
to be Miſcarriages, with which I have been Chargea-
ble ?* Yet more particularly, *What Signal thing
ſhall I do, to Save Others from Diſhonouring the Great
God by ſuch Miſcarriages, as I my ſelf once fell into.*
I will Study ſuch Things. Perhaps, the Sincerity and Conſolation of *Repentance,* cannot be better Studied, than by ſuch a conduct.

You ſhall give me leave, to preſs this one

more *Point of Prudence* upon you. There are not a few Perfons, who have many *Hours of Liefure* in the way of their *Perfonal Callings.* When the *Weather* takes them off their Bufinefs, or when their *Shops* are not full of Cuftomers, they have *Little* or *Nothing* to do; Now, Sirs, the PROPO- SAL is, *Be not Fools,* but *Redeem* this *Time* to your own Advantage, to the beft Advantage. To the *Man of Liefure,* as well as to the *Minifter,* it is an Advice of Wifdom, *Give thy felf unto Read- ing.* Good 𝕭𝖔𝖔𝖐𝖘 of all Sorts, may Employ your *Liefure,* and Enrich you with Treafures more valuable, than thofe, which the way and Work of your Callings would have purchafed. Let the baneful *Thoughts of Idlenefs* be chafed out of our Minds. But then alfo, Let Some Thoughts on that Subjed, *What Good may I do?* come into them. When you have *Liefure* to think on that Subjed, you can have no *Excufe* for not thinking on it.

§ II. THE *Ufeful Man* may now with a very good Grace, Extend and Enlarge the *Sphere* of his confideration. My next PRO- POSAL now fhall be; Let every Man confider the 𝕽𝖊𝖑𝖆𝖙𝖎𝖔𝖓, wherein the Soveraign God has placed him, and let him *Devife what Good he may do,* that may render his *Relatives,* the Better for him. One Great way to prove our felves *Really Good,* is to be *Relatively Good.* By This, more than by any thing in the World, it is, that we *Adorn the*

the Doctrine of God our Saviour. It would be an *Excellent Wisdom* in a man, to make the *Interest* he has in the Good Opinion and Affection of *any One,* an *Advantage* to do Good Service for God upon them : He that *has a Friend* will show himself indeed *Friendly,* if he think, *Such an One Loves me, and will hearken to me ; what Good shall I take advantage hence to perswade him to ?*

This will take place more particularly, where the Endearing Ties of *Natural Relation* do give us an *Interest.* Let us call over our several *Relations,* and let us have *Devices* of Something that may be called *Heroical Goodness,* in our Discharging of them. Why should we not, at least Once or Twice in a *Week,* make this *Relational Goodness,* the Subject of our *Enquiries,* and our *Purposes ?* Particularly, Let us begin with our *Domestick Relations ;* and *Provide for those of our own House ;* Lest we *Deny* some Glorious Rules and Hopes of our Christian *Faith,* in our Negligence.

First ; In the 𝕮𝖔𝖓𝖏𝖚𝖌𝖆𝖑 𝕽𝖊𝖑𝖆𝖙𝖎𝖔𝖓, how agreeably may the *Conforts* think on those Words ; *What knowest thou, O Wife, whether thou shalt Save thy Husband ?* Or, *How knowest thou, O Man, whether thou shalt Save thy Wife ?*

The 𝕳𝖚𝖘𝖇𝖆𝖓𝖉 will do well to think ; *What shall I do, that my Wife may have cause for ever to Bless God, for bringing her unto me ?* And, *What shall I do that in my Carriage towards my Wife, the Kindness of the Blessed JESUS towards His Church, may be followed and resembled ?* That this Questi-

D 3   on

on may be the more perfectly anſwered, Sir, Sometimes ask her to help you in the Anſwer ; Ask her to tell you, what ſhe would have you to do.

But then, the **Wife** alſo will do well to think ; *Wherein may I be to my Husband, a Wife of that Character* ; She will do him Good, and not Evil, all the Dayes of his Life ?

With my *Married People,* I will particularly leave a Good Note, which I find in the Memorials of *Gervaſe Diſney* Eſq. *Family-Paſſions, cloud Faith, diſturb Duty, darken Comfort.* You'l do the more Good unto one another, the more this Note is thought upon. When the *Husband* and *Wife* are always contriving to be *Bleſſings* unto one another, I will ſay with *Tertullian, Unde Sufficiam ad Enarrandam fælicitatem Ejus Matrimonii !* O Happy Marriage *!*

Parents, Oh ! How much ought you to be continually *Deviſing,* and even *Travailing,* for the *Good* of your *Children.* Often *Deviſe* ; How to make them *Wiſe Children* ; How to carry on a Deſireable *Education* for them ; an *Education* that ſhall render them Deſireable ; How to render them Lovely, and Polite Creatures, and *Serviceable* in their Generation. Often *Deviſe,* How to Enrich their Minds with Valuable *Knowledge* ; How to Inſtil Generous, and Gracious, and Heavenly *Principles* into their Minds ; How to Reſtrain and Reſcue them from the *Pathes of the Deſtroyer,* and fortify them againſt their

their *Special Temptations.* There is a World of *Good,* that you have to Do for them. You are without *Bowels,* Oh! be not such *Monsters*! if you are not in a continual Agony to do for them all the *Good* that ever you can. It was no mistake of *Pacatus Drepanius* in his Panegyric to *Theodosius ; Instituente Natura Plus fere Filios quam nosmetipsos diligimus.*

I will Prosecute this Matter, by Transcribing a Copy of PARENTAL RESOLUTIONS, which I have some-where met withal.

I. ‘ At the Birth of my Children, I would use
‘ all *Explicit Solemnity* in the *Baptismal* Dedicati-
‘ on and Consecration of them unto the LORD.
‘ I would present them to the BAPTISM of
‘ the Lord, not as a meer Formality ; but won-
‘ dring at the Grace of the Infinite GOD, who
‘ will accept *my* Children, as *His,* I would Re-
‘ solve to do all I can that they may be *His.* I
‘ would now actually Give them up unto GOD ;
‘ Entreating, that the Child may be a *Child* of
‘ God the *Father,* a *Subject* of God the *Son,* a
‘ Temple of God the *Spirit,* and be rescued from
‘ the Condition of a *Child of Wrath,* and be Pos-
‘ sessed and Employed by the Lord as an Ever-
‘ lasting Instrument of His Glory.

II. ‘ My Children are no sooner grown capa-
‘ ble of Minding the Admonitions, but I would
‘ often, often Admonish them to be sensible of
‘ their *Baptismal Engagements* to be the Lords.
‘ Often tell them, of their *Baptism,* and of what

‘ it

' it binds 'em to : Oftner far, and more times
' than there were *Drops of water,* that were caft
' on the Infant, upon that occafion !

    ' Often fay to them, *Child, You have been Baptifed* ;
' *You were wafhed in the Name of the Great God* ; *Now you*
' *muft not Sin againft Him* ; *To Sin is to do a Dirty, a*
' *Filthy thing.* Say, *Child. You muft every Day cry to God*
' *that He would be your Father, and your Saviour, and your*
' *Leader* ; *In your Baptifm He Promifed that He wou'd be*
' *fo, if you Sought unto Him.* Say, *Child, You muft Re-*
' *nounce the Service of Satan, You muft not follow the Vani-*
' *ties of this World, you muft Lead a Life of Serious Religi-*
' *on* ; *In your Baptifm you were bound unto the Service of*
' *your only Saviour.* Tell the Child ; *What is your*
' *Name* ; *you muft fooner Forget this Name, that was given*
' *you in your Baptifm, than forget that you are a Servant*
' *of a Glorious Chrift whofe Name was put upon you in your*
' *Baptifm.*

    III. ' Let my *Prayers* for my *Children* be Daily,
' with Conftancy, with Fervency, with Agony ;
' Yea, *By Name* let me mention each One of
' them, every Day before the Lord. I would
' Importunately Beg for all Suitable Bleffings to
' be beftow'd upon them ; That God would
' *Give them Grace, and give them Glory, and withold*
' *no Good Thing from them* ; That God would
' *Smile on their Education, and give His Good Angels*
' *the charge over them, and keep them from Evil, that*
' *it may not grieve them* ; That when *their Father*
' *and Mother fhall forfake them, the Lord may take*
' *them up.* With Importunity I would plead that
' Promife on their behalf; *The Heavenly Father*
' *will give the Holy Spirit unto them that Ask Him.*
                                           ' Oh !

‘ Oh ! Happy Children, If by *Asking* I may ob-
‘ tain the *Holy Spirit* for them !

IV. ‘ I would betimes entertain the Children,
‘ with Delightful *Stories* out of the Bible. In the
‘ Talk of the *Table,* I would go thro’ the *Bible,*
‘ when the *Olive-Plants about my Table* are capa-
‘ ble of being fo *Watered.* But I would always
‘ conclude the *Stories* with fome *Leffons* of Piety,
‘ to be inferred from them.

V. ‘ I would Single out Some *Scriptural Sen-*
‘*tences,* of the greateft Importance ; and Some
‘ alfo that have *Special Antidotes* in them againft
‘ the Common Errors and Vices of Children.
‘ They fhall quickly get thofe *Golden Sayings* by
‘ heart, and be rewarded with *Silver* or *Gold,* or
‘ fome Good Thing, when they do it.   Such as,

‘ *Pfal.* CXI. 10.
‘ *The Fear of the Lord, is the Beginning of Wifdom.*
‘ Matth. XVI. 26
‘ *What is a Man Profited, if he gain the whole World,*
‘ *and Lofe his own Soul.*
‘ I. Tim. I 15.
‘ *JESUS CHRIST came into the World to Save*
‘ *Sinners, of whom I am Chief.*
‘ Matth. VI. 6.
‘ *Enter into thy Clofet, and when thou haft fhut thy Door,*
‘ *Pray to thy Father which is in Secret.*
‘ Eccl. XII. 14.
‘ *God fhall bring every work into Judgment, with every*
‘ *Secret thing.*
‘Eph. V 25.
‘ *Put away Lying, Speak every One the Truth.*
‘ Pfal.

' Pſal. CXXXVIII. 6

' *The Lord hath Reſpect unto the Lowly, but the Proud*
' *He knows afar off.*

' Rom. XII. 17, 19.

' *Recompence to no One Evil for Evil. Dearly beloved,*
' *Avenge not your ſelves.*

' Neh XIII. 18.

' *They bring Wrath upon Iſrael, by Profaning the*
' *Sabbath.*

' A Jewiſh Treatiſe quoted by *Wagenſeil,* tells
' us, That among the Jews, when a Child began
' to Speak, the Father was bound to teach him
' that verſe : Deut. 33. 4. *Moſes Commanded us a*
' *Law, even the Inheritance of the Congregation of*
' *Jacob.* Oh! Let me betimes make my Chil-
' dren acquainted with the Law which our Blef-
' ſed JESUS has *Commanded* us ! Tis the beſt
' *Inheritance* I can derive unto them.

VI. ' I would betimes cauſe my Children to
' Learn the *Catechiſm.* In *Catechiſing* of them, I
' would break the Anſwer into many Leſſer and
' Proper *Queſtions;* and by their Anſwer to them
' Obſerve and Quicken their *Underſtandings.* I
' would bring every *Truth,* into ſome *Duty* and
' *Practice,* and Expect them to *Confeſs* it, and *Con-*
' *ſent* unto it, and *Reſolve* upon it. As we go on
' in our *Catechiſing,* they ſhall, when they are a-
' ble, Turn to the *Proofs,* and *Read* them, and ſay
' to me, *What* they prove, and *How.* Then, I
' will take my times, to put nicer and harder
' *Queſtions* to them ; and improve the Times of
' Converſation with my Family, (which every
' man

'man ordinarily has or may have, for confe-
'dences on matters of Religion.

VII. ' Reftlefs would I he, till I may be able to
'Say of my *Children, Behold, They Pray* ! I would
' therefore Teach them to *Pray.* But after they
'have Learnt a *Form of Prayer,* I will prefs them,
'to proceed unto Points which are not in their
' *Form.* I will fhow them the *State of their own*
' *Souls ;* and on every Stroke Enquire of them,
' *What they think ought now to be their Prayer.* I
' will direct them, that every Morning they
' fhall take one Text or Two out of the *Sacred*
' *Scripture,* and Shape it into a *Defire,* which they
' fhall add unto their *Ufual Prayer.* When they
' have heard a *Sermon,* I will mention to them
' over again the main Subject of it, and ask them
' thereupon, *What they have now to Pray for.* I
' will charge them, with all poffible cogency, to
' *Pray in Secret ;* And often call upon them,
' *Child, I hope, You don't forget my charge to you,* a-
' *bout Secret Prayer: Your crime is very great, if you do !*

VIII. ' I would betimes do what I can, to be-
' get a *Temper of Benignity* in my *Children,* both
' towards one another, and towards all other Peo-
' ple. I will inftruct them how Ready they
' fhould be to *Communicate unto others,* a part of
' what they have ; and they fhall fee, my En-
' couragements, when they difcover a *Loving,* a
' *Courteous,* an *Helpful* Difpofition. I will give
' them now and then a piece of Money, for them
' with their own Little Hands to difpenfe unto
' the

' the Poor. Yea, if any one has *hurt* them, or
' *vex'd* them, I will not only forbid them all *Re-*
' *venge*, but alſo oblige them to do a *Kindneſs* as
' ſoon as may be to the *Vexatious* Perſon. All
' *Coarſeneſs* of *Language* or *Carriage* in them, I will
' diſcountenance it.

IX. ' I would be Sollicitous to have my *Chil-*
' *dren* Expert, not only at *Reading* handſomely,
' but alſo at *Writing* a fair Hand. I will then
' aſſign them ſuch *Books* to *Read,* as I may judge
' moſt agreeable and profitable ; obliging them
' to give me ſome Account of what they *Read ;*
' but keep a Strict Eye upon them, that they
' don't Stumble on *the Devils Library,* and poiſon
' themſelves with fooliſh *Romances,* or *Novels,* or
' *Playes,* or *Songs,* or *Jeſts that are not convenient.*
' I will ſet them alſo, to *Write* out ſuch things,
' as may be of the greateſt Benefit unto them ;
' and they ſhall have their Blank Books, neatly
' kept on purpoſe, to Enter ſuch Paſſages as I
' adviſe them to. I will particularly require
' them now and then, to *Write* a *Prayer* of their
' own Compoſing, and bring it unto me ; that
' ſo I may diſcern, what ſenſe they have of their
' own Everlaſting Intereſts.

X. ' I Wiſh that my *Children* may as ſoon as
' may be, feel the Principles of *Reaſon* and *Honour,*
' working in them, and that I may carry on
' their Education, very much upon thoſe Princi-
' ples. Therefore, firſt, I will wholly avoid, that
' harſh, fierce, crabbed uſage of the Children,
' that

' that would make them Tremble, and Abhor to
' come into my Prefence. I will fo ufe them,
' that they fhall *fear* to offend me, and yet migh-
' tily *Love* to fee me, and be glad of my coming
' home, if I have been abroad at any time. I
' would have it Look'd upon as a Severe and
' Awful *Punifhment* for a crime in the Family,
' To be *forbidden for a while to come into my Pre-*
' *fence.* I would raife in them, an High Opinion
' of their Fathers *Love* to them, and of his being
' *better able* to Judge what is Good for them, than
' they are for themfelves. I would bring them
' to Believe, *Tis beft for them to be and do as I*
' *would have them.* Hereupon I would continu-
' ally Magnify the matter to them, What a brave
' thing 'tis to *Know* the things that are Excel-
' lent ; and more brave to *Do* the things that are
' Vertuous. I would have them to propofe it as
' a *Reward* of their Well-doing at any time, *I*
' *will now go to my Father, and he will teach me*
' *fomething that I was never taught before.* I would
' have them afraid of doing any *Bafe* Thing,
' from an horrour of the *Bafenefs* in it. My firft
' Animadverfion on a Leffer Fault in them, fhall
' be a *Surprife,* a *Wonder,* vehemently Exprefs'd
' before them, that ever they fhould be guilty
' of doing fo foolifhly ; a vehement *Belief,* that
' they will never do the like again ; a Weeping
' Refolution in them, that they will not. I will
' never difpenfe a *Blow,* except it be for an atro-
' cious Crime, or for a leffer Fault Obftinately
' per-

' perſiſted in ; either for an Enormity, or for an
' *Obſtinacy.* I would ever *Proportion* chaſtiſements
' unto Miſcarriages ; not Smite bitterly for a
' very ſmall piece of *Childiſhneß,* and only frown
' a little for ſome real *Wickedneß.* Nor ſhall my
' *Chaſtiſements* ever be diſpenſed in a *Paſſion* and
' a *Fury* ; but with them, I will firſt ſhow them
' the Command of GOD, by Tranſgreſſing
' whereof they have diſpleaſed me. The Slaviſh,
' Raving, Fighting way of Education too Com-
' monly uſed, I look upon it, as a conſiderable
' Article in the Wrath and Curſe of God, upon
' a miſerable World.

XI. ' As ſoon as we can, weel' get up to yet
' *Higher Principles.* I will often tell the *Children,*
' What cauſe they have to *Love* a Glorious *CHRIST,*
' who has *Dy'd* for them. And, How much He will
' be *Well-pleaſed* with their *Well-doing.* And, what
' a Noble Thing, 'tis to follow His *Example* ;
' which *Example* I will deſcribe unto them. I
' will often tell them, That the *Eye of God* is up-
' on them ; the Great GOD Knowes all they
' do, and Hears all they Speak. I will often tell
' them, That there will be a Time, when they
' muſt appear before the *Judgment-Seat* of the
' Holy LORD ; and they muſt *Now* do nothing,
' that may *Then* be a Grief & Shame unto them.
' I will Set before them, The Delights of that
' *Heaven* that is prepar'd for Pious Children ; and
' the Torments of that *Hell* that is prepared of
' old, for naughty ones. I will inform them, Of
' the

' the *Good Offices* which the *Good Angels* do for
' *Little Ones* that have the Fear of God, and are
' afraid of Sin. And, how the *Devils* tempt
' them to do Ill Things; how they hearken to
' the *Devils*, and are like *them*, when they do
' such things; and what mischiefs the *Devils* may
' get leave to do them in this World, and what
' a Sad thing t wil be, to be among the *Devils* in
' the *Place of Dragons*. I will cry to God, That He
' *will make them feel the Power of these Principles.*

XII ' When the *Children* are of a Fit Age for
' it, I will sometimes *Closet* them; have them
' with me *Alone*; Talk with them about the State
' of their Souls; their *Experiences*, their *Proficien-*
' *cies*, their *Temptations*; obtain their Declared
' Consent unto every Stroke in the *Covenant of*
' *Grace*; and then Pray with them, and Weep
' unto the Lord for His *Grace*, to be bestow'd up-
' on them, and make them Witnesses of the Ago-
' ny with which I am *Travailing* to see the I-
' mage of CHRIST formed in them. Certain-
' ly, They'l never forget such Actions!

XIII. ' I would be very Watchful and Cauti-
' ous, about the *Companions* of my *Children*. I
' will be very Inquisitive, what *Company* they
' keep; If they are in hazard of being Ensnared
' by any *Vicious Company*, I will earnestly pull them
' out of it, as *Brands out of the Burning*. I will
' find out, and procure, *Laudable Companions*
' for them.

XIV. ' As in *Catechising* the Children, so in the
' *Re-*

' *Repetition* of the Publick Sermons, I would ufe
' this Method. I will put every *Truth* into a
' *Queftion*, to be anfwered ftill, with, *Yes*, or, *No.*
' By this Method, I hope to Awaken their *Atten-*
' *tion* as well as Enlighten their *Underftanding.*
' And thus I fhall have an Opportunity to ask,
' *Do you Defire fuch or fuch a Grace of God ?* and the
' like. Yea, I may have Opportunity to De-
' mand, and Perhaps to *Obtain* their Early, and
' Frequent, and why not *Sincere ? Confent* unto
' the glorious Articles of the *New Covenant.* The
' *Spirit of Grace* may fall upon them in this Action ;
' and they may be Siez'd by Him, and Held as
' His *Temples*, thro' Eternal Ages.

 XV. ' When a Day of *Humiliation* arrives, I
' will make them know the *Meaning* of the Day.
' And after Time given them to confider of it,
' I will order them to tell me ; *What Special Af-*
' *flictions they have met withal ?* And, *What Good*
' *they hope to get by thofe Afflictions ?* On a Day
' of *Thanksgiving*, they fhall alfo be made to
' know the *Intent* of the Day. And after confi-
' deration, they fhall tell me, *What Mercies of God*
' *unto them they take Special Notice of* : And, *What*
' *Duties to God, they Confefs and Refolve, under fuch*
' *Obligations ?* Indeed, For Something of this
' Importance, to be purfued in my Converfati-
' on with the Children, I would not confine my
' felf unto the *Solemn Dayes*, which may occur
' too feldom for it. Very particularly, when
' the *Birth-dayes* of the Children anniverfarily
          ' arrive

‘ arrive to any of them, I would then take them
‘ afide, and mind them of the *Age,* which *having*
‘ *obtained Help from* God they are come unto ;
‘ How *Thankful* they fhould be for the Mercies of
‘ God, which they have hithetto Liv’d upon ;
‘ How *Fruitful* they fhould be in all Goodnefs,
‘ that fo they may ftill enjoy their Mercies. And
‘ I would enquire of them, whether they have
‘ ever yet Begun to Mind the *Work* which God
‘ fent them into the World upon ? How far they
‘ underftand the work ; And what Good Strokes
‘ they have Struck at it ? And, How they defign
‘ to Spend the Reft of their Time, if God ftill
‘ continue them in the World ?

XVI. ‘ When the *Children* are in any *Trouble,*
‘ as, if they be *Sick,* or *Pain’d,* I will take Advan-
‘ tage therefrom, to Set before them the Evil of
‘ *Sin,* which brings all our *Trouble ;* and how
‘ fearful a Thing it will be to be caft among the
‘ *Damned,* who are in Eafelefs and Endlefs *Trou-*
‘ *ble.* I will Set before them the benefit of an
‘ Intereft in a CHRIST, by which their *Trouble*
‘ will be Sanctified unto them, and they will be
‘ prepared for *Death,* and for Fulnefs of Joy in an
‘ Happy Eternity after *Death.*

XVII. ‘ I incline, that among all the Points of
‘ a Polite Education which I would endeavour
‘ for my *Children,* they may each of them, the
‘ *Daughters* as well as the *Sons,* have fo much In-
‘ fight into fome *Skill,* which lies in the way of
‘ *Gain,* (the *Limners,* or the *Scriveners,* or the
E ‘ *Apo-*

' *Apothecaries*, or Some other *Mystery*, to which
' their own Inclination may moſt carry them,)
' that they may be able to Subſiſt themſelves, and
' get ſomething of a Livelihood, in caſe the Pro-
' vidence of God ſhould bring them into Neceſ-
' ſities. Why not they as well as, *Paul the Tent-*
' *Maker*! The *Children* of the beſt Faſhion, may
' have occaſion to bleſs the Parents, that make
' ſuch a Proviſion for them! The Jews have a
' Saying ; Tis worth my Remembring it. *Qui-*
' *cunque Filium ſuum non docet opificium, perinde eſt*
' *ac ſi eum doceret Latrocinium.*

XVIII. ' As ſoon as ever I can, I would make
' my Children apprehenſive of the main END,
' for which they are to *Live ;* that ſo they may
' as ſoon as may be, *begin to Live ;* and their
' *Youth* not be nothing but *Vanity.* I would ſhow
' them, that their main END muſt be, *To Ac-*
' *knowledge the Great* GOD, *and His Glorious*
' CHRIST ; *and bring Others to Acknowledge Him :*
' And that they are never *Wiſe* nor *Well*, but
' when they are doing ſo. I would ſhow them,
' what the *Acknowledgments* are, and how they are
' to be made. I would make them able to Anſwer
' the Grand Queſtion, *Why they Live ; and what*
' *is the End of the Actions that fill their Lives ?*
' Teach them, How their *Creator* and *Redeemer* is
' to be Obey'd in every thing ; and, How every
' thing is to be done in *Obedience* to Him; Teach
' them, How even their *Diverſions*, and their
' *Ornaments*, and the *Tasks* of their Education,
' muſt

' muſt all be to fit them for the *further Service* of
' Him, to whom I have devoted them; and how
' in theſe alſo, His Commandments muſt be the
' Rule of all they do.   I would ſometimes there-
' fore Surprize them with an Enquiry, *Child,*
' *What is this for? Give me a Good Account, Why you*
' *do it?* How comfortably ſhall I ſee them *Walk-*
' *ing in the Light,* if I may bring them *Wiſely* to
' anſwer this Enquiry; and what *Children of the*
' *Light?*
     XIX. ' I would oblige the *Children,* to Retire
' ſometimes, and Ponder on that Queſtion; *What*
' *ſhall I wiſh to have done, if I were now a dying?*
' And Report unto me, their *own Anſwer* to the
' Queſtion; Of which I would then take Ad-
' vantage, to inculcate the *Leſſons of Godlineſſ* up-
' on them.   I would alſo Direct them and Ob-
' lige them, at a proper Time for it, Seriouſly
' to Realize, their own Appearance before the
' awful *Judgment-Seat* of the Lord JESUS
' CHRIST, and Conſider, *What they have to*
' *Plead, that they may not be ſent away into Everlaſt-*
' *ing Puniſhment? What they have to Plead, that they*
' *may be Admitted into the Holy City?*   I would
' inſtruct them, What *Plea* to prepare; Firſt,
' Show them, how to get a part in the *Righte-*
' *ouſneſſ* of Him that is to be their *Judge;* by Re-
' ceiving it with a Thankful *Faith,* as the *Gift* of
' infinite Grace unto the Diſtreſſed and Unwor-
' thy Sinner: Then, Show them how to prove
' that their *Faith* is not a counterfeit, by their
E 2   ' con-

‘ continual Endeavour to pleafe Him in all things,
‘ who is to be their *Judge,* and to Serve His King-
‘ dom and Intereft in the World. And I would
‘ charge them, to make this preparation.

XX. ‘If I Live to fee the Children *Mar-*
‘ *riageable,* I would, before I confult with
‘ Heaven and Earth for their beft Accom-
‘ modation in the *Married State,* Endeavour
‘ the *Espousal* of their Souls unto their only
‘ *Saviour.* I would as plainly, and as fully as I
‘ can, propofe unto them, the Terms on which
‘ the Glorious Redeemer would *Espouse* them to
‘ Himfelf, *in Righteousness and Judgment, and Fa-*
‘ *vour, and Mercies for ever;* and Sollicit their
‘ Confent unto His Propofals and Overtures.
‘ Then would I go on, to do what may be Ex-
‘ pected from a Tender Parent for them, in their
‘ *Temporal Circumstances.*

From thefe *Parental Resolutions,* how *Naturally,*
how *Reasonably* may we pafs on to Say?

Children, The *Fifth* *Commandment* confirms
all your other Numberlefs and Powerful Obligations, often to *Devise, Wherein may I be a Blessing*
to my Parents? Ingenuity would make this the very
Top of your *Ambition;* To be a *Credit,* and a
Comfort of your *Parents;* to *Sweeten,* and if it
may be, to *Lengthen* the *Lives* of thofe, from
whom, under God, you have received *your Lives.*
And *God the Rewarder* ufually gives it, even *in this*
Life, a moft obfervable Recompence. But it is
poffible, you may be the Happy Inftruments of
more

more than a little *Good* unto the *Souls* of your
Parents ; [will you Think, *How* !] Yea, tho'
they fhould be Pious Parents, you may by fome
Exquifite Methods, be the Inftruments of their
Growth in Piety, and in Preparation for the Heavenly World.   O *Thrice and Four times Happy Children* !   Among the Arabians, a Father fometimes
takes his Name from an Eminent SON, as well
as a Son from his Reputed Father.   A Man is
called with an *Abu,* as well as an *Ebn.*   Verily,
A Son may be fuch a Blefling to his Father that
the beft Sir-name for the glad Father would be,
The Father of fuch an One-

Mafters, Yea, and **Miftreffes** too, muft
have their *Devices, How to Do Good unto their Servants ;* How to make them the *Servants* of
Chrift, and the *Children* of God.   God whom you
muft Remember to be *Your Mafter in Heaven,* has
brought them, and put them into your Hands.
Who can tell what *Good* He has brought them for ?
How if they fhould be the *Elect* of God, fetch'd
from *Africa,* or the *Indies,* and brought into your
Families, on purpofe, that by the means of their
being *There,* they may be brought home unto the
Shepherd of Souls ?   Oh ! That the *Souls* of our
Slaves, were of more Account with us ! That we
gave a better Demonftration that we *Defpife not
our own Souls,* by doing what we can for the *Souls*
of our *Slaves,* and not ufing them as if they had
no *Souls* ! That the poor *Slaves* and *Blacks,* which
Live with us, may by our means be made the

Can-

Candidates of the Heavenly Life ! How can we pretend unto *Chriſtianity,* when we do no more to *Chriſtianize* our *Slaves*! Verily, you muſt give an *Account* unto God, concerning *them.* If they be Loſt, thro' your Negligence, what Anſwer can you make unto *God the Judge of all* ! Me-thinks, common Principles of Gratitude ſhould incline you, to Study the Happineſs of thoſe, by whoſe Obſequious Labours, your Lives are ſo much accommodated. Certainly, They would be the *Better Servants* to you, the more Faithful, the more Honeſt, the more Induſtrious, and Sub-miſſive *Servants* to you, for your bringing them into the Service of your *Common Lord.*

But if any Servant of God, may be ſo honoured by Him, as to be made the Succeſsful Inſtru-ment, of obtaining from a *Britiſh* Parlaiment, *An Act for the Chriſtianizing of the Slaves in the Plantations* ; then it may be hoped, ſomething more may be done, than has yet been done, that the *Blod of Souls* may not be found in the *Skirts* of our Nation: A *Controverſy* of Heaven with our Colonies may be removed, and *Proſperity* may be reſtored ; Or, however the honourable In-ſtrument, will have unſpeakable *Peace* and *Joy,* in the Remembrance of his Endeavours. In the mean time, the *Slave-Trade* is a Spectacle that Shocks *Humanity.*

> *The harmleſs Natives baſely they trepan,*
> *And barter Baubles for the Souls of men.*

The

The Wretches they to Chriſtian Climes bring o'er
To ſerve worſe Heathens than they did before.

I have ſomewhere met with a Paper under
this Title, The RESOLUTION of a MASTER;
which may here afford an agreeable Paragraph
and Parentheſis.

    I. ' I would always Remember, that my *Servants*
' are in ſome ſort my *Children.* In a Care, *That they*
' *may want nothing that may be good for them,* I would
' make them as my *Children.* And, as far as the *Methods*
' *of Inſtilling Piety,* which I uſe with my *Children,* may
' be Properly and Prudently uſed with theſe, they
' ſhall be Partakers in them. Nor will I leave them
' Ignorant of any thing, wherein I may *Inſtruct* them
' to be uſeful in their Generation.

    II. ' I will ſee that my *Servants* be furniſhed with
' *Bibles,* and Able and Careful to *Read* the *Lively Ora-*
' *cles.* I will put both *Bibles* and other Good and Fit
' Books into their Hands ; and allow them *Time* to
' *Read,* but aſſure my ſelf that they don't *Miſpend* this
' Time. If I can diſcover any *Wicked Books* in their
' Hands, I will take away from them, thoſe
' Peſtilential *Inſtruments of Wickedneſs.* They ſhall
' alſo *Write* as well as *Read,* if I can bring them to it.
' And I will ſet them now and then ſuch Things to
' *Write,* as may be for their greateſt Advantage.

    III. ' I will have my *Servants* preſent at the Religi-
' ous Exerciſes of my *Family* ; and let fall either in the
' *Speeches,* or in the *Prayers,* of the *Daily Sacrifice* in the
' Family, ſuch Paſſages, as may have a Tendency to
' quicken a Senſe of Religion in them.

    IV. ' The *Catechiſing* Stroke as far as the *Age*
' or *State* of the *Servants* will permit, that it may be
' done

' done with Decency, fhall Extend unto them alfo.
' And they fhall be concerned in the *Conferences*,where-
' in the Repetition of the Publick Sermons, may en-
' gage me with my *Family.* If any of them, when
' they come to me, have not Learnt the *Catechifm*, I
' will fee to it, that they fhall do it; and give them a
' *Reward* when they have done it.

V. ' I will be very *Inquifitive* and *Sollicitous* about
' the *Company* chofen by my *Servants* ; and with all
' poffible Cogency refcue them from the Snares of
' *Evil Company* : forbid their being the *Companions of*
' *Fools.*

VI. ' Such of my *Servants* as may be Employ'd for
' that purpofe, I will Employ to Teach *Leffons of Piety*
' unto my *Children* ; and Recompenfe them for doing
' fo. But I would with a particular *Artifice* contrive
' them to be fuch *Leffons*, as may be for their own E-
' dification too.

VII ' I will fometimes call my *Servants* alone ; Talk
' with them about the *State of their Souls* ; Tell them
' how to clofe with their only *Saviour* ; Charge them
' to Do well, and *Lay hold on Eternal Life* ; And fhow
' them very Particularly, how they may render all
' the *Service* they do for *me*, a Service to the Glorious
' *Lord*; how they may do all from a Principle of O-
' bedience to the Lord, and become Intitled unto the
' *Reward of the Heavenly Inheritance.*

I make this Appendix to thefe RESOLUTI-
ONS. I have read fuch a Paffage as this.

' *Age* is well nigh fufficient with fome *Mafters* to ob-
' literate every Letter and Action, in the Hiftory of
' a Meritorious Life ; and *Old Services* are generally
' buried under the Ruines of an *Old Carcafe.* And
this Paffage, ' Its a barbarous Inhumanity in men to-
' wards their Servants, to make their fmall Failings to
' be

' be a Crime, without allowing their paſt Services to
' have been a Vertue. *Good God, keep thy Servant from
ſuch Ingratitude* ! Worſe than *Villianous* Ingratitude !

But then, O 𝕾𝖊𝖗𝖛𝖆𝖓𝖙𝖘, If you would arrive to the *Reward of the Inheritance,* You ſhould
Set your ſelves to *Deviſe ; How ſhall I approve my
ſelf ſuch a Servant, that the Lord may Bleſs the Houſe
of my Maſter, the more for my being in it ?* Certainly, There are many wayes, wherein *Servants*
may be *Bleſſings.* Let your *Studies* with your continual *Prayers* for the welfare of the *Families* to
which you belong, and the *Example* of your So-
ber Carriage, render you ſuch. If you will remember but *Four Words,* and Endeavour all that
is comprized in them, OBEDIENCE, HONES-
TY, INDUSTRY, and PIETY, you will be the
Bleſſings and the *Joſephs* of the Families to which
you belong. Let thoſe Four Heads, be diſtinctly & frequently thought upon. And go cheerfully through all you have to do, upon this conſideration ; *That it is an Obedience to Heaven, and
from thence will have a Recompence.* It was the Obſervation even of a Pagan, *That a Maſter may receive a Benefit from a Servant.* And, *Quod fit af-
fectu Amici, deſinit eſſe Miniſterium.* It is a *Friend-
ſhip* rather than a *Service, Young man,* if it be
with the Affection of a *Friend,* that you do what
you do for your *Maſter.* Yea, Even the *Maid-
Servants* in the Houſe, may do an unknown *Service* to it, by Inſtructing the *Infants,* and Inſtilling

ftilling the *Leſſons of Goodneſs* into them. So, by *Bilhab,* and *Zilpah,* may Children be *Born again*; The *Miſtreſſes* may by the *Travail* of their *Maid-Servants,* have *Children,* brought into the King-dom of God.

I will go on. *Humanity* teaches us, to take Notice of all that are our *Kindred. Nature* be-ſpeaks, that which we call a *Natural Affection* to all that are *Akin* to us. To be without it, is a very Bad Character; 'tis a Brand on the worſt of *Men*; on ſuch as forfeit the Name of *Men.* But now, *Chriſtianity* is to Improve it. Our *Natural Affection* is to be improved into a *Religious Inten-tion.* Sir, Take a Catalogue of all your more 𝔇𝔦𝔰𝔱𝔞𝔫𝔱 𝔯𝔢𝔩𝔞𝔱𝔦𝔳𝔢𝔰. Conſider them One after another; and make every one of them, the Subjects of your *Good Devices.* Think ; *Wherein may I purſue the Good of ſuch a Relative?* And, *By what means may I render ſuch a Relative the better for me?* It is poſſible, you may do ſomething, that may give them cauſe to Bleſs God, that ever you have been *Related* unto them. Have they no *Calamity,* under which you may give them ſome Relief? Is there no *Temptation* a-gainſt which you may give them ſome Caution? Is there no Article of their *Proſperity,* to which you may be Subſervient? At leaſt ; with your affectionate *Prayers,* you may go over your *Ca-talogue* ; You may Succeſſively Pray for every One of them all by Name ; And, if you can, Why ſhould you not alſo put agreeable *Books of of Piety* into their Hands, to be Lasting *Remem-bancers* of their *Duties* to God, and of your *Desires* for them ?

§ 12. MEthinks, This Excellent Zeal should be carried into our *Neighbourhood.* *Neighbours,* You stand *Related* unto One another; And you should be full of *Devices,* That all the *Neighbours* may have cause to be glad of your being in the *Neighbourhood.* We read, *The Righteous is more Excellent than his Neighbour.* But we shall scarce own him so, Except he be *more Excellent* AS *a Neighbour.* He must *Excell* in the Duties of *Good Neighbourhood.* Let that man be *Better* than his *Neighbour,* who Labours to be a *Better Neighbour;* to Do most *Good* unto *his Neighbour.*

And here, first; The *Poor* People that ly *Wounded,* must have *Wine* and *Oyl* poured into their *Wounds.* It was a charming Stroke in the Character with a Modern Prince had given to him, *To be in Distress, is to deserve his Favour.* O Good Neighbour, put on that Princely, that more than Royal Quality. See who in the Neighbourhood may *Deserve thy Favour.* We are told, *This is Pure Religion and Undefiled;* (A Jewel, that neither is a counterfeit, nor has any Flaws in it :) *To Visit the Fatherleß and Widows in their Affliction.* The *Orphans* and the *Widows,* and so all the Children of *Affliction* in the Neighbour-hood,

hood, muſt be *Viſited*, and Relieved with all a-
greeable Kindneſſes.

Neighbours, Be concerned, That the *Orphans*
and *Widows* in your Neighbourhood, may be
well provided for. *They* meet with grievous Difficulties; with unknown Temptations. While
their next *Relatives* were yet Living, they were,
perhaps, but meanly provided for. What muſt
they now be in their more Solitary condition?
Their condition ſhould be conſidered : And the
Reſult of the conſideration ſhould be that; *I
delivered the Orphan, that had no Helper, and I cauſed
the Heart of the Widow to Sing for Joy.*

By conſequence, All the Afflicted in the Neighbourhood, are to be thought upon. Sirs, Would
it be too much for you, at leaſt *Once in a Week?*
To Think, *What Neighbour is reduced into a Pinch-
ing and Painful Poverty? Or in any Degree Im-
poveriſhed with heavy Loſſes?* Think, *What Neighbour is Languiſhing with Sickneſs; Eſpecially if Sick
with ſore Maladies, and of ſome Continuance?* Think,
*What Neighbour is Heart-broken with ſad Bereave-
ments; Bereaved of Deſireable Relatives?* And
Think; *What Neighbour has a Soul buffeted, and
hurried with violent Aſſaults of the Wicked one?* But
then Think, *What ſhall be done for ſuch Neighbours.*

Firſt, You will *Pitty* them. The Evangelical
Precept is, *Have Compaſſion One of another, Be Pit-
tiful.* It was of old, and ever will be, the juſt
Expectation, *To him that is Afflicted, Pitty ſhould
be ſhown.* And let our *Pitty* to them, flame out
in

in our *Prayer* for them. It were a very Lovely Practice for you, in the *Daily Prayer* of your *Closet* every Evening, to think, *What miserable Object have I seen to day, that I may do well now to mention for the Mercies of the Lord ?*

But this is not all. 'Tis possible, 'tis probable, you may do well to *Visit* them ; and when you *Visit* them, *Comfort* them. Carry them some *Good Word,* which may raise a *Gladness,* in an *Heart Stouping with Heaviness.*

And lastly. Give them all the *Assistences* that may answer their *Occasions* : Assist them with *Advice* to them ; Assist them with *Address* to others for them. And if it be needful, Bestow your 𝕬𝖑𝖒𝖘 upon them ; *Deal thy Bread to the Hungry ; Bring to thy House the Poor that are cast out ; when thou seest the Naked, Cover him.* At least, *Nazianzens* Charity, I pray ; *Si nihil habes, da Lacrymulam*; If you have nothing else to bestow upon the Miserable, bestow a *Tear* or two upon their Miseries. This *Little,* is better than *Nothing* !

Would it be amiss for you, to have alwayes lying by you, a List of the *Poor* in your Neighbourhood, or of those whose *Calamities* may call for the *Assistences* of the Neighbourhood ? Such a *List* would often furnish you, with Matter for an *Useful Conversation,* when you are Talking with your Friends, whom you may *Provoke to Love and Good Works.*

I will go on to say ; Be Glad of *Opportunities*
to

to *Do Good* in your *Neighbourhood:* Yea, look out for them, lay hold on them, with a rapturous Affiduity. *Be Sorry* for all the *Bad Circumstances* of any Neighbour, that bespeak your *doing of Good* unto him. Yet, *Be Glad*, if any one tell you of them. Thank him who tells you, as having therein done you a very great Civility. Let him know, that he could not by any thing have more gratified you. Any *Civility* that you can show, by *Lending*, by *Watching*, by ---- all the Methods of *Courtesie*; Show it; and be glad you can Show it. Show it, and give a *Pleasant Countenance*, [*Cum munere Vultum,*] in the Showing of it. Let your *Wisdom* cause your *Face* always to *Shine*; Look, not with a *Cloudy* but a Serene and *Shining Face*, upon your Neighbours; and Shed the Rayes of your *Courtesy* upon them, with such Affability, that they may see they are Welcome to all you can do for them. Yea, Stay not until you are told of *Opportunities* to *Do Good.* Enquire after them; Let the Enquiry be Sollicitous, be Unwearied. The Incomparable Pleasure, is worth an Enquiry.

There was a generous Pagan, who counted a *Day Lost*, if he had obliged no body in the Day. *Amici, Diem Perdidi!* O *Christian*, Let us try, whether we can't attain to Do Something, for Some Neighbour or other, every day that comes over our Head. Some do So; and with a better Spirit, than ever *Titus Vespasian* was acted withal. Thrice in the Scriptures, we find the
Good

Good Angels *Rejoycing* : 'Tis alwayes, *At the Good of Others*. To *Rejoyce* in the *Good* of Others, and moſt of all in doing of *Good* unto them, 'tis *Angelical Goodneſs*.

In moving for the *Devices* of *Good Neighbourhood*, a principal motion which I have to make, is ; That you Conſult the *Spiritual* Intereſts of your Neighbourhood, as well as the *Temporal*. Be concerned, Leſt the *Deceitfulneſs of Sin* undo any of the Neighbours. If there be any *Idle Perſons* among them, I beſeech you, cure them of their *Idleneſs* ; Don't nouriſh 'em & Harden 'em in That ; but find *Employment* for them. Find 'em *Work* ; Set 'em to *Work* ; Keep 'em to *Work*. Then, as much of your other Bounty to them, as you pleaſe.

If any *Children* in the Neighbourhood, are under no Education, don't allow 'em to continue ſo. Let care be taken, that they may be better Educated ; and be taught to Read ; and be taught their *Catechiſm* ; and the Truths and Wayes of their only Saviour.

Once more. If any in the Neighbourhood, are taking to *Bad Courſes*, Lovingly & Faithfully Admoniſh them. If any in the Neighbourhood are Enemies to their own Welfare, or their Families ; Prudently diſpenſe your Admonitions unto them. If there are any *Prayerleſs Families*, never leave off Entreating and Exhorting of them, till you have perſwaded them, to Set up the *Worſhip* of God. If there be any *Service* of God, or of His People, to which any
one

one may need to be Excited, give him a Tender
Excitation. Whatever *Snare* you see any one in,
be so kind, as to tell him of his Danger to be *Ensnared,* and Save him from it. By putting of
Good Books into the Hands of your Neighbours,
and gaining of them a Promise to *Read the Books,*
who can tell, what Good you may do unto
them ! It is possible, you may in this way, with
Ingenuity, and with Efficacy, administer those
Reproofs, which you may owe unto such Neighbours, as are to be *Reproved* for their Miscarriages.
The *Books* will balk nothing, that is to be said,
on the Subjects, that you would have the Neighbours advised upon.

Finally. If there be any *Base Houses,* which
threaten to debauch, and Poison, and confound
the Neighbourhood, Let your Charity to your
Neighbours, make you do all you can, for the
suppression of them.

That my PROPOSAL *To Do Good in the Neighbourhood, and as a Neighbour,* may be more fully
formed and followed ; I will conclude it, with
minding you, That a World of *Self-Denial* is to
be Exercised in the Execution of it. You must
be armed against *Selfishness,* all *Selfish* and *Squinting*
Intentions, in your generous Resolutions. You
shall see how my Demands will grow upon you.

First. You must not think of making the *Good*
you do, a pouring of Water into a Pump, to draw
out something for your selves. This might be
the meaning of our Saviours Direction ; *Lend,*
Hoping

Hoping for nothing again. To *Lend* a Thing, properly is to *Hope* that we shall *Receive it again.* But this probably refers to the, Εραυισμ℗, Or, *Collation,* usual among the Ancients, whereof we find many Monuments and Mentions in Antiquity. If any Man by Burnings, or Shipwrecks or other Disasters, had lost his Estate, his Friends did use to *Lend* him considerable Sums of Money, to be Repaid, not at a certain Day, but when he should find himself Able to Repay it, without Inconvenience. Now, they were so cunning, that they would rarely *Lend* upon such Disasters, unto any but such, as they had *Hope,* would Recover out of their present Impoverishment, and not only Repay them their Money, but also Αντεραυιζειν *Requite* their Kindness, if ever there should be need of it. The thing required by our Saviour, is, *Do Good unto such as you are never like to be the Better for.*

But then, there is yet an Higher Thing to be demanded, That is ; *Do Good* unto those Neighbours who have *Done Hurt* unto you. So sayes our Saviour, *Love your Enemies, Bless them that Curse you, Do Good to them that Hate you, and Pray for them which despitefully use you and persecute you.* Yea, If an *Injury* have been done you, improve it as a provocation to do a *Benefit* unto him who did the *Injury.* This is Noble. T'wil bring marvellous Consolations ! Another Method might make you *Even* with your Froward Neighbours ; This, will Set you *Above* them all. T'were Nobly

F   done,

done, If in the clofe of the Day, when you are Alone before the Lord, you make a *Particular Prayer*, for the Pardon and Profperity, of any Perfon, from whom you may have fuffered any Abufe in the Day. And it would be Nobly done, If at laft calling over the *Catalogue* of fuch as have been Abufive to you, you may be able to fay, [the only Intention that can juftify your doing any thing like to keeping a *Catalogue* of them!] *There is not one of thefe, but I have done him, or watch'd to do him, a Kindnefs*! Among the *Jews* themfelves, there were the *Hafideans*, One of whofe Inftitutions it was, To make this Daily Prayer unto God, *Remitte et condona omnibus qui Vexant nos. Chriftians,* go beyond them. Yea, *Juftin Martyr* tells us, In the Primitive Times they did fo ; ὑπὲρ τῶν ἐχθρῶν εὐχόμενοι, *Praying for their Enemies.*

But I won't Stop here. There is yet an Higher Thing to be demanded. That is ; *Do Good* unto thofe Neighbours, who will *Speak Ill* of you, after you have done it. So fayes our Saviour ; *Ye fhall be the Children of the Higheft ; He is kind unto the Unthankful, and unto the Evil.* You will every day find, I can tell you, *Monfters of Ingratitude.* Yea, if you *diftinguifh* any Perfon, with Doing for him, fomething more than you have done for others, it will be well if that very Perfon do not at fome time or other, hurt you wonderfully. Oh! the *Wifdom* of *Divine Providence*, in ordering this Thing ! Sirs, It is, that you may *Do Good*

on

on a *Divine Principle* ; *Good*, meerly for the Sake
of *Good*! *Lord, Increase our Faith* !

And God forbid, that a *Christian Faith*, should
not come up to a *Jewish* ! There is a Memorable
Passage, in the *Jewish* Records. ' There was a
' Gentleman, of whose Bounty many People eve-
' ry day received Reliefs and Succours. **One**
' day he asked ; *Well, What do our People say to day* ?
' They told him, *Why, The People partook of your*
' *Kindnesses, and Services, and then they Bless'd you*
' *very fervently*. Did they so, Said he ; *Then I*
' *shall have no Great Reward for this Day.* Another
' Day he asked, *Well, And what say our People now* ?
' They told him, *Alas, Good Sir, the People Enjoy'd*
' *your Kindnesses to day, and when all was done, they*
' *did nothing but Rail at you.* Indeed ! Said he ;
' *Now for this Day I am sure that God will give me*
' *a Good and Great Reward.*

Tho' vile Constructions, and harsh Invectives,
be never so much the *Present Reward* of doing
the best Offices for the Neighbourhood, yet, my
Dear *Boniface* ; Be victorious over all Discourage-
ments : *Thy Work shall be well Rewarded, saith the*
Lord !

If your Opportunities to *Do Good* reach no
further, yet I will offer you a Consolation, which
One has Elegantly thus Expressed. *He that*
Praises God only on a Ten-stringed Instrument, with
his Authority Extending but unto his Family, and his
Example but unto his Neighbourhood, may have as
Thankful an heart here, and as high a Place in the

Cælestial

Cæleſtial Choir hereafter, as the greateſt Monarch, that Praiſeth God upon a Ten thouſand ſtring'd Inſtrument. Upon the Loud ſounding Organs, having as many Millions of Pipes as there be People under him.

§ 13. HOw can we leave the offices of *Good Neighbourhood*, without Interpoſing a PROPOSAL, To Animate and Regulate 𝔓𝔯𝔦𝔳𝔞𝔱𝔢 𝔐𝔢𝔢𝔱𝔦𝔫𝔤𝔰 of *Religious* People, *for the Exerciſes of Religion* ? It is very certain, That where ſuch *Private Meetings* under a Good Conduct, have been kept Alive, the Chriſtians which have Compoſed them, have like ſo many *Coals of the Altar* kept one another Alive, and kept up a lively Chriſtianity in the Neighbourhood. Such *Societies* have been tried and ſtrong Engines, to uphold the *Power of Godlineß.* The Throwing up of ſuch *Societies*, has been accompanied with a viſible *Decay of Godlineß* ; the Leſs *Love* to them, the Leſs *Uſe* of them, there has been in a Place, the Leſs has *Godlineſs* flouriſhed there ; the Leſs there has been of, *The Kingdom of God.*

The *Rules* Obſerved by Some, 𝔄𝔰𝔰𝔬𝔠𝔦𝔞𝔱𝔢𝔡 𝔉𝔞𝔪𝔦𝔩𝔦𝔢𝔰, may be offered on this occaſion with ſome Advantage. They will tell us what *Good* may be done by ſuch *Societies* in a Neighbourhood.

I. It is to be propoſed. That about a dozen *Families*, more or leſs, of a Vicinity, Agree to Meet (the Men and their Wives) at each others Houſes, once in a Fortnight, or a Month, at ſuch a Time as may be
                                              Agreed

Agreed upon, and Spend a convenient Quantity of Time together, in the *Exercises of Religion.*

II. The *Exercises of Religion* proper for a *Meeting,* are ; For the Brethren to Begin and Conclude with 𝔓𝔯𝔞𝔶𝔢𝔯𝔰 in their Turns; For 𝔓𝔰𝔞𝔩𝔪𝔰 to be Sung ; And for 𝔖𝔢𝔯𝔪𝔬𝔫𝔰 to be Repeated

III. It were defireable, for the 𝔐𝔦𝔫𝔦𝔰𝔱𝔢𝔯𝔰 now and then, to afford their Prefence at the Meeting, and *Pray* with them, and *Inftruct* them, and *Exhort* them, as they may fee occafion.

IV. The *Candidates* of the Miniftry may do well, to perform fome of their *Firft Services* here, and here Shape and Mould themfelves for *Further Services.*

V. One Special *Defign* of the *Meeting,* fhould be, with *United Prayers,* to Ask the Bleffings of Heaven on the Family where they are Affembled, as well as on the reft : That with the wondrous Force of *United Prayers,* *Two or Three may agree on Earth,to ask fuch things,* as are to be done for theFamilies,by *ourFather which is in Heaven.*

VI. Such a *Meeting* fhould Look upon themfelves, as bound up in One *Bundle of Love* ; and count themfelves obliged, in very Clofe and Strong Bonds, to be Serviceable unto one another. If any one in the Society fhould fall into *Affliction,* all the reft fhould prefently Study to Relieve and Support the Afflicted Perfon, in all the wayes imaginable. If any one fhould fall into *Temptation,* the reft fhould Watch over him, and with the *Spirit of Meeknefs,* with the *Meeknefs of Wifdom,* Endeavour to Recover him. It fhould be like a *Law of the Medes and Perfians* to the whole Society, That they will upon all juft occafions, Lovingly *Give,* and as Lovingly *Take,* mutual Admonitions of any thing that they may fee *Amifs* in one another.

VII. And it is not eafy to reckon up the *Good Offices,* that fuch a *Society* may do to many, many others, as

well

well as to the *Members* whereof it is it self compofed, The *Prayers* of fuch well-difpofed *Societies,* may fetch down marvellous Favours from Heaven on their *Paftors,* whofe *Lives* may be prolonged, and *Gifts* augmented, and *Graces* brightened, and *Labours* profpered, in anfwer to the Supplications of fuch Affociated Families ; And the *Interefts of Religion* may be mightily preferved and promoted in the *whole Flock,* by their Fervent Supplications ; and the *Spirit of Grace* mightily poured out upon the Rifing Generation. Yea, *All the Land* may fare the better for them.

VIII. Efpecially, when a *Society* fhall fet apart, *whole Days* for *Prayer* with *Fafting* before the Lord, as it may be proper for them to do now and then upon fome occafions. The *Succefs* of fuch *Dayes* has been fometimes very marvellous : and the *Savour* of them, left on the Minds of the Saints, who have carried them on, has been fuch, as notably to prepare them, to *Show forth the Death of the Lord* at His Holy Table ; Yea, to *Meet with their own Death,* when God pleafes to order it.

IX. It is very fure, The *Devotions* firft, and afterwards the *Conferences,* carried on in fuch a *Society,* will not only have a notable Tendency to produce the *Comfort of Love* in the Hearts of Good Men toward One another ; But alfo their *Abilities* will be thereby Sharpened and Quickened ; they will be rendred more *Able,* to Serve many valuable Interefts.

X. Unexpected *Opportunities to Do Good,* will arife unto fuch a *Society* : But efpecially, if a Practice of this importance were once taken up ; That the MEN who Compofe the *Society,* would now and then Spend half an Hour together by themfelves, in Confidering on that Queftion, 𝔚𝔥𝔞𝔱 𝔊𝔬𝔬𝔡 𝔦𝔰 𝔱𝔥𝔢𝔯𝔢 𝔱𝔬 𝔟𝔢 𝔡𝔬𝔫𝔢 ?
More Particularly ;
Who are to be called upon, to do their Duty, in coming to Special Ordinances ?
Who

*Who is in any Special Adversity; and what shall be done
to Comfort them?*

*What Contention or Variance may there be among any
Neighbours, and what may be done for the Healing of it?*

*What Open Miscarriages do any Live in; and who shall
be desired to carry Faithful Admonitions unto them?*

Finally; *What is there to be done for the Advantage,
and Advancement of our Holy Religion?*

In the Primitive Times of Christianity there
was much use made of a Saying, which they
ascribed unto *Matthias* the Apostle; Εαν εκλεκτν
ſειτων αμαρτηση, ημαρτεν ο εκλεκτος. *If the Neighbour of
an Elect, or Godly, Man Sin, the Godly Man himself has also Sinned.* The Obligations of Neighbours Watchfully to *Admonish* one another, were
what that Saying intended. Oh! how much
may *Christians Associated* in Religious Combinations, do by Watchful and Faithful Admonitions,
to prevent being *Partakers in other Mens Sins* !

The Man, that shall produce, and promote
such *Societies,* will do an unknown deal of Good
in the *Neighbourhood.*

And so will he, that shall help forward another
Sort of 𝕊𝕠𝕔𝕚𝕖𝕥𝕚𝕖𝕤 ; namely, those of 𝕐𝕠𝕦𝕟𝕘
𝕄𝕖𝕟 𝔸𝕤𝕤𝕠𝕔𝕚𝕒𝕥𝕖𝕕.

These duely managed, have been incomparable *Nurseries* to the *Churches,* where the Faithful
Pastors have countenanced them. *Young Men*
are hereby *Preserved* from very many *Temptations,*
Rescued from the *Pathes of the Destroyer,* Confirmed in the *Right Wayes of the Lord,* and Prepared

mighti'y

mightily for such *Religious Exercises* as will be Expected from them, when they come themselves to be *Housholders.*

I will make a Tender of some ORDERS, which have been observed in some such *Societies.*

I. Let there be *Two Hours* at a Time Set apart; and, Let there be *Two Prayers* made by the Members of the *Society,* in their *Turns* ; Between which, Let a *Sermon* be Repeated; And there may be the Singing of a *Psalm* annexed.

II. Let all the Members of the Society, Resolve to be *Charitably Watchful* over one another : Never to divulge one anothers Infirmities ; Alwayes to inform and advise one another of every thing that may appear to call for an Admonition, and to take it Kindly when they are Admonished.

III. Let all who are to be admitted as Members of the *Society,* be accompanied by Two or Three of the rest, unto the *Minister* of the Place, that they may recieve his Holy Counsils, and Charges, and that every thing may be done with his Approbation ; and so let their *Names* be added unto the *Roll.*

IV If any Person thus *Enrolled* among them, fall into a *Scandalous Iniquity* Let the Rebukes of the *Society* be dispensed unto him ; and let them Forbid him to come any more among them, until he bring Suitable Expressions and Evidences of *Repentance* with him.

V. Let the *List* be once a Quarter called over ; and then, if it be Observed, that any of the *Society* have much absented themselves, Let there be Some sent unto them, to Enquire the Reason of the Absence ; and if no Reason be given, but such as intimates an *Apostasy* from Good Beginnings, Let them upon Obstinacy, after Loving and Faithful Admonitions, be Obliterated.

VI, Once

VI. Once in Three Months, Let there be, if Need be, a *Collection,* out of which the Neceffary Charges of the *Society* fhall be Defray'd, and the reft be Employ'd upon fuch Pious Ufes, as may be agreed upon

VII. Once in *Two Months,* Let the whole Time of the Meeting, be Devoted unto Supplications, for the Converfion and Salvation of the *Rifing Generation* in the Land ; and Particularly, for the Succefs of the Gofpel, in that Congregation, whereto the *Society* does belong.

VIII. Let the whole *Society,* be Exceedingly careful, that their Difcourfe while they are together, after the other Services of Religion are over, have nothing in it, that fhall have any Taint of *Backbiting* or *Vanity,* or the leaft Relation to the affairs of *Government,* or to things which do not concern them, and do not Serve the Interefts of Holinefs in their own Converfation. But let their Difcouafe be wholly on the Matters of Religion ; and thofe alfo, not the Difputable and Controverfal Matters, but the Points of *Practical Piety.* They may propofe *Questions* upon this Intention, and every one in an orderly manner, take his liberty to *Anfwer* them. Or, They may go thro' the *Catechifm,* and One at One time, another at another, hear all the reft recite the *Anfwers* thereof Or, They may otherwife be directed by their *Paftors,* to fpend their Time together profitably.

IX. Let every Perfon in the *Society,* look upon it, as a Special Task incumbent on him, to Look out, for fome other hopeful *Young man,* and ufe all proper pains, to Engage him in the Refolutions of Godlinefs, until he alfo fhall be joyned unto the *Society.* And when a *Society* fhall in this way be increafed unto a fit Number, Let it *Swarm* into *More* ; who may hold an ufeful correfpondence with one another.

The

The Man, who shall be the Instrument of Setting up such a *Society* in a Place, cannot comprehend, unto what a Long and Rich Train of Good consequences, he is become Instrumental.

And they that shall in such a *Society* together carry on the Duties of Christianity, and the Praises of a glorious CHRIST, will have upon themselves, a blessed Symptom, that they shall be together Associated in the *Heavenly City*, and in the Blessedness that shall never have an end.

§ 14. HItherto my Discourse has been a more *General Address*, unto People of all Conditions and Capacities. I have proposed few *Devices*, but those, upon which Persons in *Private* Circumstances, as well as others, may be discours'd unto. We will proceed now to those that are in more *Publick* Circumstances. And, first, Because no men in the World are under such Obligations to *Do Good*, as the 𝕸𝖎𝖓𝖎𝖘𝖙𝖊𝖗𝖘 𝖔𝖋 𝖙𝖍𝖊 𝕲𝖔𝖘𝖕𝖊𝖑, *It is necessary that the Word of God should be first spoken unto* THEM.

Will my Fathers and Brethren, Give me Leave. Certainly, They that are *Men of God*, should be *alwayes at Work for God* ! Certainly, They that are *Dedicated* unto the Special Service of the Lord, should never be satisfyed, but when they are in the most sensible Manner Serving Him. Certainly, They whom the *Great King* has brought nearer to Himself than other men, should be more unwearied than any men, in Endeavours to advance
vance

vance His *Kingdom.* They whom the Word of God calls *Angels,* ought certainly to be of an *Angelical Difpofition ;* Difpofed evermore to *Do Good,* like the *Good Angels ; Minifters* always on the Wing to *do His Pleafure.* Tis no improper PROPOSAL, That they would Serioufly Set themfelves to think, *What are the Points wherein I fhould be Wife and Do Good, like an Angel of God ? Or, If an Angel were in Flefh, as I am, and in fuch a Poft as I am, what Methods may I juftly imagine, he would ufe to Glorify God ?* What wonderful Offices, of *Kindnefs,* and with how much *Delight,* would the *Good Angels* do, for fuch their *Fellow-Servants* ! We muft call upon our People, *To be Ready to Every Good Work.* We muft Go before them in it ; By our own *Readinefs at Every Good Work,* fhow them how. *Timothy, Be thou an Example of the Believers !* It is a true Maxim, and you cannot think too often upon it ; *The Life of a Minifter, is the Life of his Miniftry.* And there is another Maxim like unto it, *The Sins of Teachers are the Teachers of Sins.*

Allow me, Sirs. Your *Opportunities to Do Good,* are Singular. Your want of Worldly *Riches,* and of any way ordinarily to get 'em, is compenfated by the *Opportunities to Do Good,* which you are *Enriched* withal. The true *Spirit of a Minifter,* will caufe you to count your felves *Enriched,* when thofe precious things are conferred upon you, and to prize them above any *Farms,* or *Bags,* or whatever Temporal Poffeffions.

In

In operibus fit Abundantia mea ; Divitijs per me Licet, abundet, quifquis voluerit. Well Struck, Brave *Melanĉthon !*

'Tis to be hoped, That the Main Principle that aĉted you, when you firſt Entred upon the *Evangelical Miniſtry,* was, *An Hope to do Good in the World.* If that principle were then too feeble in its operation, 'tis Time that it ſhould now o- perate, and that you ſhould now Vigorouſly aĉt upon it, and that the *Zeal* thereof ſhould now *Eat up* your Time, your Thought, your All.

That you may be *Good Men,* and be mightily Inſpired and Aſſiſted from Heaven to *Do Good,* it is needful that you ſhould be *Men of Prayer.* I lay this down to be allow'd, as my very Firſt *Poſtulatum !* In the Purſuance of this Intention, there appears more than a little Need of it, That you ſhould ever now and then Keep whole *Dayes of Prayer,* in an Holy Retirement before the Lord; Often Set apart, whole *Dayes,* for *Prayer with Faſting,* in Secret, and perfume your Studies with *Devotions Extraordinary :* and uſually with a Mixture of *Alms,* to go up in the *Memorial* be- fore the Lord. By ſuch *Dayes,* you may obtain, with the Pardon of your *Unfruitfulneſs,* for which, alas, how often have we cauſe to repair unto the Great *Sacrifice !* --- You may obtain, I ſay, a vaſt Improvement in *Piety* and *Sanĉtity;* which is, of how vaſt Conſequence, to make an *Uſeful Mini- ſter !* *Sanĉtify them in,* (or for) *thy Truth,* ſayes our Saviour. They ſhould be *Sanĉtifyed,* that
would

would be Inftruments for the Propagation of the *Truth.* You may obtain, a certain *Afflatus* from Heaven upon your Minds,and fuch an *Indwelling of the Holy Spirit*, as will render you, Grave, Difcreet, Humble, Generous,and *Men* worthy to be *Greatly Beloved.* You may obtain thofe Influences from above, that will Difpel the *Enchantments*, and Conquer the *Temptations*, which may elfe do a World of Mifchief in your Neighbourhood. You may obtain *Direction* and *Affiftence* from Heaven, for the many Services to be done, in your Difcharge of your Miniftry. Finally, You may fetch down unknown *Bleffings* on your Flocks, and the whole People for which you are to be *the Lords Remembrancers.*

Your *Publick Prayers* well compofed and well adapted, will be Excellent *Engines* to *do Good.* The more Judicious, the more Affectionate, the more Argumentative, you are in them,the more you will *Teach your People to Pray.* Yea, I befeech you, Sirs ; How can you profecute any *Intention of Piety* among your People more Effectually, than by Letting them fee you Praying, and Weeping, and Striving, and in an Importunate Agony before the Lord, that you may gain it for them ?

The more Significantly you reprefent the *Various Cafes* of your People in your *Publick Prayers* ; the more devoutly fenfible you will make them of their own cafes. And it will wonderfully comfort them !

The

The *Prayers* made at *Baptifms*, may be fo ma.
naged, as mightily to awaken in all People, the
Confcience of their Baptifmal Obligations.

What effufions of the *Holy Spirit*, may your
People feel, if your Prayers at the *Table* of the
Lord, are, as *Nazianzen* I remember fayes, his
Fathers were ; *Made by the Holy Spirit of God* !

Your *Sermons*, if they be *Well-Studied*, as from
the confideration of their being *Offerings* unto
God, *the Great KING*, as well as unto His People, they ought to be, will *Do Good* beyond all
Expreffion. The manner of your *Studying* them,
is that which may much contribute unto it. It is
needful, that you Study the *Condition* of your
Flocks ; and bring them fuch *Truths*, as will notably *Suit* their prefent circumftances. In order
to this, You will obferve their *Condition*, their
Faults, their Snares, their Griefs, that you may
Speak a word in Seafon ; and if any thing Remarkable Fall out, you will Suit the *Words* to the
Works of God. You may Divide your People
into *Claffes* ; and think, What Leffons of Piety,
you are to Difpenfe, unto the *Communicants*,
what, unto all that are under the *Bonds of the Covenant* ; what, unto the *Aged* ; what unto the
Worldly ; what unto the *Rich* ; what unto the *Poor*
what unto them that are in *Offices* ; what unto
them that are under Such, and Such *Afflictions*
what in regard of Peoples *Perfonal Callings*. A-
bove all, The *Young* muft not be forgotten : Yet
evill Employ all the *Tunes* imaginable, to raife

Early

Early Piety. Yea, You may do well to let it be understood, that you would willingly be advised, by any *Perfons*, or *Meetings*, in your Flocks, what *Subjects* they may want or wish to hear Treated on ; By giving them *Sermons* on such *Subjects*, you at leaft very much Edify thofe who have asked for them ; and it is probable, very many more.

And, what if while you are Studying your *Sermons*, You fhould at the clofe of every Paragraph, make a *Paufe*, and Endeavour with *Acknowledgements* and *Ejaculations* to Heaven, and with *Self-Examinations*, to feel fome Impreffions of the *Truths* in that Paragraph on your own Souls, before you go any further ? By fuch a Practice, the *Hours* which you take, to Make and Write a *Sermon*, will prove fo many *Hours of Devotion* with you. The *Day* in which you have made a *Sermon* will even leave upon your Mind, fuch a Savour as a *Day of Prayer* ufes to do. When you come to Preach the Sermon, you will do it with great Liberty and Affurance ; and the *Truths* thus prepared will be likely to come with a more Senfible Warmth and Life upon the Auditory ; *From the Heart, and To the Heart* ! A famous Preacher would fay, *I Never durft Preach a Sermon to others, till I have got firft fome Good by it my felf.* And I will add, *That is the way for it to do much Good unto others.* Let fuch a *Rabbi*, be called, our *Hadarfan* ! [or, The *Preacher* !] Let the Saying of the Ancient be Remembred ; *Qui Ludit*

in

in Cathedra Lugebit in Gehenna. And the Saying of a Modern alfo, not be forgotten ; *Cold Preachers make Bold Sinners.*

But then, Sirs, Your 𝕬𝕾𝕾𝕾𝕾; Oh ! how much may you do for CHRIST among your People in them! It is Pitty but that you fhould impofe it as a Law upon your felves ; *Never to make an Unprofitable Vifit.* Even when you render a Pure *Vifit* of *Civility*, or for *Diverfion*, 'tis eafy for you, to keep this Law ; *That you will drop fome Speech or other, Good for the ufe of Edifying, before you leave the Company.* There have been *Paftors* able to fay, They Scarce ever once went into an Houfe among their People in their Lives, without fome Effay or Purpofe to *Do Good* in the Houfe, be-fore they came out of it.

The fame Rule would be very well obferved with fuch as *Come* unto us, as well as with thofe whom we *Go* unto. Why fhould any of our People ever come anear us, without our con-triving, *To Speak fomething to them that may be ufe-ful to them !* Our *Peter Martyr* having been ma-ny Dayes in *Bucers* Houfe, Publifhed this Report of it. *Aufim affirmare, me ab illius Menfa, femper difceffiffe Doctiorem.* I make no Doubt, That the Obfervation of this Rule, may be very confiftent with an *Affable*, yea, and, as far as is *Convenient*, a *Facetious* Converfation. Tho' *Quæ funt in ore populi Nugæ, funt in ore facerdotis Blafphemiæ.*

But, Sirs, In your *Vifits*, you will take a parti-cular Notice of the *Widow*, the *Orphan*, the *Afflicted*; and

and carry all agreeable Reliefs unto them. The *Bills* put up in your Congregations, will a little help you, to find out, who need your *Visits.*

If any *Special Calamity* hath befallen any One, 'tis a Time to *Visit* them, with very particular *Directions* and *Perswasions* unto them, to hear the *Voice of God* in the Calamity ; to comply with the *Intent* and *Errand*, which it comes upon.

If any One has received any *Special Deliverance,* tis a Time to *Visit* them, and therein to perswade them, that they will think of some *Singular Thing,* to be done by way of Thankfulness for their Deliverance ; and not leave them, till the Thing be Agreed and Resolv'd upon.

The *Handmaids of the Lord,* that are near their *Lying in,* may on this account be very proper objects for your *Visits.* At such a Time they are in much distress ; the approaching *Hour of Trouble* threatens to be their *Dying Hour.* The Counfils that will Exactly instruct them how to prepare far a *Dying Hour,* will now if ever, be attentively hearkened unto. And there are precious *Promises* of God, which they should also be taught now to Live upon. To bring them these *Promises* will do the work, and give you the Welcome, of a *Good Angel* unto them.

CATECHISING, is a Noble Exercife ; it will infenfibly bring you into a way to *Do Good,* that Surpaffes all Expreffion. Your *Sermons* will be very much loft upon an *Uncatechifed People.* Nor will your People Mind fo much, what you

G   Speak

Speak to them in the Pulpit, as what you Speak to them in the more *Approaching* and *Familiar* way, of Applying the Anſwers of the *Catechiſm.* Never any *Miniſter,* that was a *Great Catechizer* did Repent of it; Thouſands, Thouſands ! have bleſs'd God, with Wonders & Praiſes, for the good Succeſs of it.   The moſt *Honourable Man of God,* ſhould reckon it, no Abaſement or Abatement of his Honour, to Stoup unto this *Way of Teaching.* Yea, ſome Eminent Paſtors, in their Emerited *Old Age,* when other Labours have been too hard for them, have, like the famous old *Gerſon,* wholly given themſelves up to *Catechiſing ;* Tho' there have been others of whom that brave Chancellour of *Paris,* in his Treatiſe, *De Pueris ad Chriſtum trabendis,* makes a ſad complaint ; *Adeo jam indignum videtur apud Multos, ſi quis ex Theologis, aut famatus in Literis, vel Eccleſiaſtica Dignitate Prædites, ad hoc opus ſe inclinaverit.*

The Methods of carrying on this Exerciſe, will be varied by the *Paſtors,* who ſo *Love* a Glorious CHRIST, as to mind His Word, *Feed my Lambs ;* according to the Varieties of their circumſtances.

But Some have choſen the way of 𝔓𝔞𝔰𝔱𝔬𝔯𝔞𝔩 𝔘𝔦𝔰𝔦𝔱𝔰.   And from the Memorials of One who long ſince did ſo, and then left his, 𝔓𝔞𝔱𝔢𝔯𝔫𝔞, to his *Son* upon it, I will tranſcribe the Enſuing Paſſages.

For, 𝔓𝔞𝔰𝔱𝔬𝔯𝔞𝔩 𝔘𝔦𝔰𝔦𝔱𝔰.

' You

' You may set upon *Visiting* all the Families, be-
' longing to your Flock ; taking *One Afternoon* in a
' Week for that Purpose.

' You may still send before hand unto the *Families,*
' that you intend at such a Time to *Visit* them. And
' when you come unto them ; you may assay with as
' Handsome and as Pungent Addresses as you are able,
' to treat every Person particularly about their Ever-
' lasting Interests.

' First, You may discourse with the *Elder* People
' upon such Points as you think most proper for them.

' And especially, charge them to Maintain *Family-*
' *Prayer* ; and Obtain their Promises for it, if they have
' yet neglected. Yea, Now *Pray with them,* that you
' may show them *how to Pray,* as well as to obtain their
' Purposes for it.

You may likewise press upon them, the Care of In-
' structing their *Children* and *Servants,* in the Holy Re-
' ligion of our *Saviour;* and to bring them up for Him.

' If any that you should have Spoken with, were
' Absent. you may frequeutly Leave a Solemn Text or
' Two of the *Sacred Scripture,* which you think most a-
' grecable for them ; Desiring Some-body present,
' That they would Remember you Kindly to them.
' and from you Recommend unto them *that Oracle* of
' God.

' You may then call for the *Children* and *Servants ;*
' And putting unto them such *Questions* of the *Catechism,*
' as you think fit, you may, from the *Answers,* make as
' lively Applications unto them, as you can, for the
' Engaging of them unto the Fear of God.

' You may frequently get *Promises* from them, rela-
' ting to *Secret Prayer,* and *Reading* of the *Scriptures,* and
' *Obedience* to their *Parents* and *Masters.*

' And you may frequently Set before them the *Pro-*

G 2

' *poſals* of the New Covenant, after you have Laboured
' for their Conviction & Awakening ; till with Floods
' of Tears,they Expreſsly Declare their Conſenting to,
' and Accepting of, the *Propoſals* of the *Covenant of*
' *Grace,* which you diſtinctly ſet before them.

'Some of the *Leſſer Folks,* you may order, to bring
' their *Bibles* unto you, and Read unto you from thence
' Two or Three Verſes, whereto you may turn them.
' This will *Try,* whether they can *Read well,*or no. You
' may then Charm them to Think on ſuch Things, as
' you thence obſerve for their Admonition, and never
' Forget thoſe *Faithful Sayings* of God.

' You may ſome times leave ſome *AwfulQueſtion* with
' them ; which, you may tell them, they ſhall not
' Anſwer to *You,* but Anſwer to *Themſelves.* As, *What*
' *have I been doing, ever ſince I came into the World, about*
' *the Great Errand upon which God ſent me into the World ?*
' And, *If God ſhould now call me out of the World, what*
' *would become of me throughout Eternal Ages ?* And,
' *Have I ever yet by Faith carried a Periſhing Soul unto my*
' *only Saviour, for both Righteouſneſs and Salvation ?*

' You will Enjoy a moſt wonderful Preſence of God
' with you, in this undertaking ; and ſeldom leave a
' *Family,* without many *Tears* of Devotion dropt by all
' ſorts of Perſons in it.

' You can ſeldome Diſpatch more than *Four* or *Five*
' Families in an Afternoon; and the work may be as
' *Laborious* as any in all your Miniſtry.

' *My Son,* I adviſe you, to ſet a ſpecial Value upon
' that part of your Miniſtry, which is to be diſcharged
' in 𝔓𝔞𝔰𝔱𝔬𝔯𝔞𝔩 𝔘𝔦𝔰𝔦𝔱𝔰. You will not only *Do,* but alſo
' *Get,* more than a little Good, by your Converſation
' with all ſorts of Perſons, in thus *Viſiting* of them *from*
' *Houſe to Houſe.* And you will never more *Walk in*
' *the Spirit,*than when you thus *Walk* about your Flock,
' to Do what Good you can among them, In

In your *Visits,* an incredible Deal of Good may be done, by diſtributing little *Books of Piety.* You may without *Great Coſt,* be furniſhed with *Little Books* to Suit all occaſions : *Books* for the *Old* and for the *Young* ; *Books* for Perſons under *Afflictions,* or under *Deſertions* ? *Books* for Perſons under the Power of ſpecial *Vices* ; *Books* for them that neglect *Houſhold Piety* ; *Books* for the *Sea-faring* ; *Books* for the *Erroneous* ; *Books* for them whom you would Quicken and Prepare to approach the *Table* of the Lord ; *Books* for them that come to have their Children *Baptiſed.* And *Catechiſms* for the Ignorant. You may notably clench your Admonitions, by Leaving agreeable *Books* in the Hands of thoſe, whom you have diſcourſed withal ; you may give them to know, that you would be looked upon as Diſcourſing by *theſe* unto them, after you are departed from them. And in this way you may Speak more than you have Time to Speak in any Perſonal Interview : Yea, ſometimes more than you would care to Speak. By Good *Books,* there is a *Salt of Piety* Scattered about a Neighbourhood.

Paſtors, Uphold and Cheriſh Good *Schools* in your Towns. But then, be prevailed withal ſometimes to *Viſit* the *Schools.*

It is a Propoſal made, by Holy Mr. *Thomas White* ; *That Able and Zealous Miniſters, might ſometimes Preach at the Schools. Becauſe the Preaching of the Word is the Converting Ordinance ; and the Children will be Obliged there to hear with more Attention*

G 3

than

than they often do in the Publick. And the Minifters might here condefcend unto fuch Expreffions, as might work moft upon them, and fuch as are not fo fit for a Publick Congregation. I have read this Account of One who was awakened by this Advice, to do fuch things as thefe ;

' At certain Times he Succeffively Vifited the *Schools.*
' When he came to a *School*, he firft made a *Prayer* o-
' ver the *Children*, as much adapted unto their Condi-
' tion, as he could make it. Then he went thro' the
' *Catechifm*; or as much of it, as he thought neceffary ;
' making the feveral *Children* to Repeat the feveral
' *Anfwers*. But he ftill broke the *Queftions*, for each Ar-
' ticle in the *Anfwers*, to be underftood by them, with
' a *Yes*, or, *No*, Expected from them. And he put fuch
' *Queftions* alfo, as would make them to fee and own
' their own *Duties*, and often to Exprefs a Refolution
' to Do their *Duties*. Then he Preached a Short *Ser-*
' *mon* to them; Exceeding Plain; on fome Suitable
' Scripture ; and with all the Artifices and Pungency
' he could ufe, to raife Attention & Affection in them.
' After this he fingled out a Number of *Scholars*, it
' may be Seven or Eight, or Ten ; and bid each of
' them turn to a certain Scripture ; which he made
' them Read unto the whole *School*; becaufe it ftill re-
' lated unto fomething as he gave them to fee by his
' brief Remarks upon it, which it particularly concer-
' ned Children to take Notice of. Then he concluded
' with a brief *Prayer*, for a Bleffing on the *School*, and
' on the *Tutors* in it.

' We are upon *Vifiting* ; You will be fure to *Vifit*
' the *Poor* as well as the *Rich* ; and often mention
' the Condition of the *Poor*, in your Converfation
' with the *Rich*. Keep, Sir, a *Lift* of 'em !

And

And think on this, The *Wind* feeds no body, yet it may turn the *Mill*, which will grind the *Corn*, that may Feed the *Poor*. In Talking with the *Rich*; you may do this for the *Poor* in your *Lift*.

But then, in Vifiting the *Poor*, you will take occafion to difpenfe your *Alms* among them. Thefe *Alms* you will, with as much contrivance as may be, make the *Vehicles*, to Convey the *Admonitions of Piety* unto them; yea, the Methods and Machines of obtaining from them, fome Engagements to perform certain *Exercifes of Piety*. All Minifters are not alike *furnifhed* for *Alms*; they fhould all be *difpofed* for them. They that have *Small Families*, or *Large Interefts*, ought to be Shining Examples of Liberality to the Poor, and powre down their *Alms* like the Showres of Heaven upon them. Yet *All* fhould Endeavour to Do *what they can* this way. What fayes *Nazianzen* of his Reverend Fathers *Alms-Deeds?* They will find, That the more they *do* (provided it be done with *Difcretion*,) the more they *may*; The *Loaves* will multiply in the *Diftribution*. Sirs, This Bounty of yours to the *Poor*, will procure a mighty Efteem and Succefs to your Miniftry. *Suadet Lingua, Jubet Vita.* T'will be an ungainfayable Demonftration, that you *Believe what you Speak*, about all the Duties of *Chriftianity*, but particularly of *Liberality*, and a *Faithful difcharge of our Stewardfhip*, and a Mind weaned from the *Love of this World*; It will demonftrate your Belief of a *Future State*. It will Vindicate you

G 4 from

from the Imputation of, *A Worldly Man* ; It will Embolden you, and Fortify you, with a great Affurance, when you call upon others, *To Do Good*, and abound in the *Sacrifices* which God *is well-pleafed* withal. *Et fic Exempla Parantur* !

You will do well to keep a Watchful Eye on the *Diforders* that may grow up and get Head, in your Neighbourhood. Among other wayes to Supprefs thofe things, you may Form *Societies for the Suppreffion of Diforders* ; Obtain a fit number of Prudent, Pious, well affected Men, to *Affociate* upon that Intention ; Employ *their* Difcretion, and *their* Activity, for your Affiftence in your Holy Purpofes.

One of the Rules given for the *Minifter*, is, *Give thy felf to Reading*. Sirs, Let *Gregories Paftoral*, & *Bowles's Paftor Evangelicus*, be fome of theBooks on which you beftow a *Reading*. But then, if you Read *Church Hiftory* very much, (and particularly, the *Prudentia Veteris Ecclefiæ*, Written by *Vedelius*,) but efpecially the *Lives* of both Ancient and Modern *Divines*, you will ever now and then find, *Methods to Do Good*, Exemplified. You will then confider, how far you may *Go and do likewife*.

How Serviceable may *Minifters* be, unto one another, and unto all the Churches, in their feveral *Affociations* ! Many things of General Advantage to all their Flocks may be advanced, and confulted there. Yea, 'Tis Pitty, that there fhould be the leaft occafional *Meeting of Minifters*
at

at any time, without *Some Useful thing* propofed in it.

Nero took it very ill, that *Veſpaſian* Slept, at his *Muſick!* It is very much, very much to be Wiſh-ed, That the Sin of *Sleeping at Sermons*, were more Watch'd againſt, and more Warn'd againſt. Your *Sleepy Hearers*, if, alas, the *Catechreſis* may be allow'd that calls them *Hearers*, do miſerably loſe the *Good* of your Miniſtry ; and the *Good* which you might, perhaps, have particularly deſign'd for them, whom at the Time of your Speaking what you prepar'd for them, you ſee Siezed with an horrible *Spirit of Slumber* before your Eyes. Will no *Vinegar* help againſt the *Narcoticks*, that Satan has given to your Poor *Eutychus's!* Or, Can't you bring that *Civility* into Faſhion among your Hearers, *To wake one another!*

Finally ; After all the Generous Eſſayes and Labours to *Do Good*, that may fill your Lives, your People will probably treat you with much *Ingra-titude.* Your *Salaries* will be meaner than even thoſe at *Geneva.* They will *Neglect* you ; they will *Oppreſs* you ; they will *Defraud* you, of what they have Engaged, and you have Expected. You have now one opportunity more to *Do Good*, and ſo to Glorify your Saviour. Your *Patience,* O Tried Servants of God, your *Patience* will do it wonderfully! To *Bear Evil* is to *Do Good*. The more *Patient* you are under *Ill Uſage*, the more you Exhibit a Glorious CHRIST unto your Peo-ple, in your conformity to your admirable Sa-viour,

viour. The more *Conformed* you are unto Him, the more *Prepared* you are, 'tis poffible, for fome Amendment of your condition in this World ; moft certainly for the Recompences of the Heavenly World, when you appear before the Lord, who fayes, *I know thy Works, and Charity, and Service, aud Faith, and thy Patience.*

I will fay This ; If to Reprefent, a Glorious CHRIST, unto the View, and Love, and Admiration of all People, be the Grant Intention of your *Lives* ; To be a *Star* that Leads men to Chrift, and Stands there ! [Ο τον χρισον εν τη ψυχη περιφερων, was the Chara&er, you know of *Ignatius*!] If you are Exquifitely Studious, that the *Holineß*, and yet the *Gentleneß*, of a Glorious CHRIST may Shine in your Converfation : If in your *Publick* Difcourfes you do with Rapture bring in the mention of a Glorious CHRIST in every Paragraph, on every Occafion, where He is to be fpoken of; and in your *Private* ones, you contrive to infinuate Something of His *Glories* and *Praifes*, where-ever it may be decently introduced ; Laftly, If when you find that a Glorious CHRIST is the more Confidered and Acknowledged by your Means, it fills you with wonderful Satisfaction ; and with *Joy Unſpeakable & full of Glory*, you now cry out ; *Lord, This is my Defired Happineß!* Truly, Sirs, You then *Live to Purpofe* ; You *Do Good* Emphatically !

There was a Worthy Minifter whom the Great Cranmer defign'd for Preferment; and he gave
this

this Account of his Defign about him ; *Nihil appetit, nihil ardet, nihil fomniat, nifi* JESUM CHRISTUM. Verily, Such *Men of Chrift*, are *Men of God.* They are the *Favourites of Heaven* ; and fhall be *Favoured* with Opportunities to *Do Good*, above any men in the World : They are the *Men whom the King of Heaven will delight to Honour* ! And they are the *Gaons* of Chriftianity.

If I referve one thing to be mentioned after *Finally*, 'tis becaufe I am in a Doubt, whether it fhould be mentioned at all. In fome *Reformed Churches*, they do not permit a *Minifter* of the Gofpel, to practife as a *Phyfician* ; Becaufe either of thofe Callings is ordinarily enough to find a full Employment for him that faithfully follows it. But, the *Priefts* of old, who referved in the Archives of their Temples, the Stories of the Cures thankfully acknowledged there ; communicated from thence Directions for cures in fuch cafes among their Neighbours. Nor has it been a rare thing it Later Ages for *Clergy men* to be *Phyficians.* Not only fuch Monks as *Ægidius Athenienfis,* and *Conftantinus Afer,* and others, who had Liefure for it ; but fuch Bifhops as *Bochelt*, yea, fuch Arch-bifhops as *Albicus,* have appeared under that Character. So, *Herbert* advifes that his *Country-Minifter,* (or at leaft, his Wife,) fhould be much of a *Phyfician* to his Flock. And we have known many a *Country Minifter* prove a vaft Bleffing to his Flock, by being fo. If a *Minifter* do any thing this way, Let

him

him for ever make it an Engine, to Addreſs the *Souls* of his People, and oblige them unto Piety. Tis an *Angelical Conjunction,* when *the Miniſters who do the Pleaſure* of CHRIST, ſhall alſo be *Phyſicians* and *Raphaels* unto their People ! In a more *Populous Place,* you will perhaps chuſe rather, Sir, to get ſome Religious and Accompliſhed *Phyſician* into your Neighbourhood ; & make *Medical Studies* your own Diverſion as much as may be ; but with ſome Eye to this, That you will Communicate unto your *Luke,* what notable Things you do in Reading meet withal ; and ſome-times *Unite Counſils* with him, for the good of his Patients. You may this way Save the *Lives* of many, who may themſelves know nothing of it.

§ 15. FRom the Tribe of *Levi,* we will paſs with our PROPOSALS to the Tribe of *Simeon* : from which Latter *Tribe,* there has been a frequent *Aſcent* into the former ; as well as a Step now and then from the former to the latter. The 𝖘𝖈𝖍𝖔𝖔𝖑-𝕸𝖆𝖘𝖙𝖊𝖗 has manifold *Opportunities* to *Do Good.* God make him ſenſible of his *Obligations*! We read, *The Little Ones have their Angels.* It is an *Hard* work to keep a *School* But it is a *Good* work ; and it may be ſo done, as to be in ſome Sort like the *Work of Angels.* The *Tutors* of the Children, may be like their *Tutelar Angels. Melchior Adam* did well to call it, *Moleſtiſſimam, ſed Deo Longe gratiſſimam Functionem.*
                                                                  Tutors,

Tutors, Will you not look upon the *Children* under your Wing as committed unto you, by the Glorious LORD, with a charge of this Importance ; *Take them, and bring them up for me, and I will pay you your Wages* ! Every time any New Children come under your Tuition, why fhould you not think ; *Here, my Glorious Lord fends me another Object, on which I may do fomething, that He may be Served in the World* ! O *Suffer Little Children to Come unto* you, and Confider, what you may do, that *Of Such may be the Kingdom of Heaven* !

Sirs, Let it be a Great Intention with you, *To Inftil Documents of Piety into the Children.* Efteem it, Your and Their Great Intereft, That they fhould So *Know the Holy Scriptures as to be made Wife unto Salvation* ; and *Know the Saviour, whom to Know is Life Eternal.* Oh ! Take all occafions to Drop Some *Honey out of the Rock* upon them ! Happy the *Children,* and as Happy the *Mafter,* where they who make the Relation of their Converfion to Serious Piety, may fay, *There was a School-Mafter that brought us to* CHRIST! You have been told ; ' Certainly, Tis a Nobler 'work, to make the Little Ones Know their ' *Saviour,* than to know their *Letters.* The Lef-' fons of *Jefus* are Nobler Things than the Lef-' fons of *Cato.* A Sanctifying *Transformation* of ' their Souls, were a Nobler Thing, than meer-' ly to conftrue *Ovids Metamorphofis.* He was a ' Good *School-Mafter,* of whom there was this ' Teftimony given. **Young**

YOung *Austin* wept, when he saw *Dido* dead ;
    Tho' not a Tear for a *Dead Soul* he had.
Our Master would not let us be so Vain,
But us from *Virgil* did to *David* train.
Textors Epiſtles would not *Cloath* our Souls ;
Pauls too we Learn't ; we *went to School at Pauls.*

CATECHISING; That ſhould be a *Frequent*, and at leaſt, a *Weekly*, Exerciſe of the *School*. And in the moſt *Edifying*, and *Applicatory* and *Admonitory* manner carried on. ' In ſome Reformed
' Places, (we are told) the Magiſtrate counte-
' nances none to keep a *School*, but what appears
' with a *Teſtimonial* of their *Ability*, and their
' *Diſpoſition* particularly, [*Aptitudinis ad munus*
' *illud imprimis puerorum Catechiſationem,*] for the
' work of *Religious Catechiſing.*

Dr. *Reynolds*, in a Funeral Sermon on an Eminent *School-Maſter* has a Paſſage worthy to be written in Letters of Gold. ' If *Grammar-Schools*
' have *Holy* and *Learned* men ſet over them, not
' only the *Brains*, but alſo the *Souls* of the Chil-
' dren might be there Enriched, and the work of
' *Learning* and of *Grace* too, be Betimes wrought
' in them. In order to this, tis to be propoſed, That you would not only *Pray* with your Scholars every day, but alſo take occaſion from the *Publick Sermons*, and from *Remarkable Occurences* of Providence in your Neighbourhood, often to inculcate the *Leſſons of Piety* upon the Children.

Tutors in the *College*, may do well Succeſſively
                                                to

to treat each of their *Pupils* alone, with all poſſible Solemnity and Affection, about their *Interior State* ; ſhow them how to Repent of *Sin*, and Believe on *Chriſt* ; and bring them to Expreſs *Reſolutions* of *Serious Piety.* Sirs, you may do a thouſand Things, to render your *Pupils Orthodox* in their Principles, *Regular* in their Practices, *Qualified* for Services !

I have read this Experiment of One who had *Pupils* under his charge ; 'He made it his Cuſtom, 'that in every *Recitation*, he would, from ſome- 'thing or other occurring in it, *make an occaſion*, ' to let fall ſome *Sentence*, which had a Tendency ' to promote the *Fear of God* in their Hearts ; ' which thing ſometimes did indeed put him to ' more than a little Study ; but the Good Effect 'Sufficiently Recompenced it.

If I ſhould Preſs for certain Authors to be made Claſſical in the *Grammar-Schools*, which are not commonly uſed there ; Such as *Caſtalio* for the *Latin* Tongue, and *Poſſelius* for the Greek ; or, if I ſhould beg, with certain Modern Writers, ' That there may be a *Northweſt Paſſage* found, for the Attaining of the *Latin Tongue* ; that in- ' ſtead of a Journey which may be diſpatch'd in ' a Few Days, they may not wander, like the ' Children of *Iſrael*, many years in the Wilderneſs : Or, if I ſhould recite *Auſtins* complaints, of Little Boys Learning the filthy Actions of the Pagan Gods in the Schools, for giving an Account whereof, ſays he, *Ob hoc bonæ Spei puer appellabar ;*

And

And *Luthers,* That our *Schools* are more Pagan
than *Christian* ; And the Reports and Wishes of
a late Writer, who sayes ; ' I knew an aged and
' famous *School-Master,* that after he had kept
' School about Fifty years, said with a sad Coun-
' tenance, That it was a great Trouble unto him,
' that he spent so much Time in Reading Pagan
' Authors to his Scholars, and wished it were
' customary to Read such a Book as *Duports* Ver-
' ses upon *Job,* rather than *Homer,* and such Books.
' I pray God, put it in the Hearts of a Wise Par-
' laiment, to *Purge our Schools* ; that instead of
' Learning Vain Fictions, and Filthy Stories,
' they may be acquainted with the Word of God,
' and with Books containing Grave Sayings, and
' things that may make them truely Wise and
' Useful in the World : I suppose, there will be
little Notice taken of such *Proposals* : I had as
good never mention them ; Tis with *Despair,*
that I make mention of them.

Among the *Occasions* to be taken for Instilling
of *Piety* into the *Scholars,* there is One peculiarly
at the *Writing-Schools.* An Inveterate Sinner I
have read of, Converted unto Serious Piety, by
accidentally seeing that *Sentence* of *Austin* written in a Window ; *He that hath Promised Pardon
to the Penitent Sinner, has not Promised Repentance to
the Presumpteous One.* Who can tell what Good
may be done to the Young Scholar, by a *Sentence* in a *Copy-book* ? Let their *Copies* be of *Sentences* worthy to be *had in Everlasting Remembrance* ;

of

of *Sentences*, that shall have the brightest *Maxims of Wisdom* in them ; Worthy to be Written on the *Fleshly Tables* of their Hearts ; to be graven with the *Point of a Diamond* there. This may do two Executions *with one Stone* : God has bless'd this unto many *Scholars*, it has done them good all their Dayes.

At the *Grammar School* also, the Scholars may be ordered for their Exercises to turn such things into *Latin*, as may be likewise for their Instruction and Establishment, in the Principles of Christianity ; and render them armed with *Supplies from the Tower of David*. Their *Epistles*, why may they not be on such *Subjects* as may most befriend Vertue in them !

I will add this ; To carry on the *Discipline of the School*, with *Rewards*, as well as *Punishments*, is most certainly very *Adviseable*, very *Preferrible*. There may be Invented many ways of *Rewarding*, the *Diligent* and the *Laudable* : And, --- *Ad Palmæ Cursurus honores*, --- a Child of any Ingenuity, under the *Expectations* and *Encouragements* of being *Rewarded*, will do to the uttermost. You have an Honour for *Quintilian*. I Pray, Hear *Quintilian ; Cavendum a Plagis, sed Potius Laude, aut aliorum Prælatione, urgendus est puer.* If a Fault must be *Punished*, Let *Instruction*, both unto the *Delinquent* and unto the *Spectator*, accompany the *Correction*. Let the *Odious Nature* of the *Sin*, that has Enforced the *Correction*, be declared ; and let nothing be done in a *Passion ;*

H all

all be done with all the Evidence of *Compaſſion* that may be.

Ajax Flagellifer may be Read at the Scool.　He is not fit for to be the Maſter of it.　Let it not be ſaid of the Scholars, They are brought up *in the School of Tyrannus.　Pliny* ſayes, That *Bears* are the Fatter for Beating.　Fitter to have the Conduct of *Bears* than of Ingenuous *Boyes,* are the Maſters, that can't give a *Bit* of Learning, but they muſt give a *Knock* with it.　Send 'em to be Tutors of the famous *Lithuanian* School, at *Samourgan.*　The Harſh, Fierce, *Orbilian* way of treating the Children, too commonly uſed in the *School,* is a dreadful *Curſe* of God upon our Miſerable Offspring, who are *Born Children of Wrath.* It is boaſted now and then of a *School-Maſter,* that ſuch and ſuch a *brave Man* had his Education under him.　There is nothing ſaid, How many that might have been *Brave Men,* have been deſtroy'd by him ; How many *Brave Wits,* have been Diſpirited, Confounded, Murdered, by his *Barbarous* way of managing them.

I have Read an Addreſs of this Importance ; and I will conclude with it, as one of Great Importance.

TUTORS, Be *Strict* ; But yet be *Gentle* too ;　
　　Don't by fierce *Cruelties* fair *Hopes* undo.　
Dream not, that they who are to Learning Slow	
Will Mend by Arguments in *Ferio.*	
Who keeps the *Golden Fleece,* Oh, Let him not	
A *Dragon* be, tho' he *Three Tongues* have got.	
　　　　　　　　　　　　　　　　　　Why

Why can you not to Learning find the way,
But thro the Province of *Severia* ?
T'was *Moderatus* who taught *Origen* ;
A *Youth* which prov'd One of the beſt of Men.
The Lads with *Honour* firſt, and *Reaſon*, rule ;
Blowes are but for the *Refractery Fool.*
But, Oh! Firſt Teach them their Great God to fear ;
An *Euge,* ſo from God and Them you'l hear.

§. 16. WE have lately diſcourſed with the PASTORS, about ſeveral Ways
to *Do Good.* There are PROPOSALS, to be
alſo laid before the CHURCHES, of matters
wherein they may do well to joyn with their
Paſtors.

𝕯𝖆𝖞𝖊𝖘 𝖔𝖋 𝖕𝖗𝖆𝖞𝖊𝖗 kept now and then by
the *Churches,* on the Declared Intention of obtaining the *Sanctifying Influences* of the Spirit of
Grace upon the Riſing Generation, have had
and would have, a marvellous Efficacy to Produce a *Religious Poſterity* in the Land ; and a
Seed accounted unto the Lord for a Generation. Such
an Acknowledgment of *Supernatural Grace* in the
Neceſſity and Excellency of it, would be a very
probable *Preparative* & *Introduction,* to the Commu-
nication of it. And when the *Children* ſee their
Parents thus Earneſtly Seeking the *Grace* of God
for them, it would have a *Natural Tendency* to a-
waken them, unto an Earneſt Seeking of it for
themſelves. The *Sermons* alſo Preached by the
Miniſters on ſuch Solemn occaſions, 'tis likely,
would be very Awakening Ones. That this
H 2   PRO-

PROPOSAL, has been fo Little hearkened unto, 'tis Lamentable, 'tis Admirable ! But --- *They
all Slumbred and Slept.*

There is another PROPOSAL, which has
been tendered to all our Churches, and attended
in Some of them.

'That the feveral Churches, having in an *Inftru-*
'*ment* Proper for that Purpofe, made a *Catalogue* of
'fuch things, as can indifputably be found amifs a-
'mong them, do with all Serioufnefs and Solemnity
'pafs their VOTES, That they count fuch things to
'be very *Offenfive Evils,* and that Renouncing all De-
'pendence on their own Strength, to avoid fuch Evils,
'they humbly Ask the Help of the *Divine Grace,*
'to Affift them in Watching againft the faid Evils,
'both in Themfelves and in One another. And that
'the *Communicants* do often Reflect upon thofe their
'𝕬𝖈𝖐𝖓𝖔𝖜𝖑𝖊𝖉𝖌𝖒𝖊𝖓𝖙𝖘 and 𝕻𝖗𝖔𝖙𝖊𝖘𝖙𝖆𝖙𝖎𝖔𝖓𝖘, as Perpetual
'𝕸𝖔𝖓𝖎𝖙𝖔𝖗𝖘 unto them, to prevent the Mifcarriages
'wherewith too many Profeffors are too Eafily over-
'taken.

It has been confidered, That fuch humble
Recognitions of Duty, will not only be Accepted
by our God, as our *Declarations* for Him, where-
upon He will Declare for us ; but alfo, they are
the *Way of the New Covenant,* for our obtaining
of Help to do our Duty. ---

A Particular *Church,* may be an illuftrious
Pillar of Truth, by confidering what Labouring
Truth, and *Part* of the Kingdom of God, may
call for Special, Signal, Open 𝕿𝖊𝖘𝖙𝖎𝖒𝖔𝖓𝖎𝖊𝖘 ;
and they may Excite their *Paftors* to the com-
pofing, and affift them in the Publifhing, of fuch

Tefti-

Teſtimonies ; and appear to accompany them in
the Action. It is likely, that God would accompany ſuch *Teſtimonies* with a marvellous Efficacy to Suppreſs growing *Errors* and *Evils* !

A PROPOSAL of this Nature may be worthy of ſome Conſideration.

I. 'IT were to be deſired, That every *Particular*
'*Church,* would be furniſhed with a STOCK,
'that may be a Conſtant and Ready 𝔉und for the
'𝔓ropagation of 𝔑eligion. And that every Mini-
'ſter would uſe his beſt Endeavours, both with his
'own Disburſements according to his Ability, and with
'his Applications unto well-diſpoſed People under his
'Influences, to increaſe the STOCK ; Either in the
'way of *Collections* Publickly made at certain Periods,
'or in the way of more Private Communications
'made from time to time unto it.

II. 'This 𝔈vangelical 𝔗reaſury may be Lodg'd
'in the Hands of the *Deacons* of each of the Churches,
'where it is gathered ; who are to keep True and
'Fair Accompts of all that is brought in and laid out.
'And let nothing be drawn out of it, without the
'Knowledge and Conſent of the *Church,* to which it
'belongs.

III. 'The Firſt and Main Intention of this 𝔈van-
'gelical 𝔗reaſury, is to be, *The Propagation of Re-*
'*ligion.* And therefore, when any Eſſayes of Good
'are to be made upon *Ungoſpellized Places,* the Neigh-
'bouring Miniſters may Adviſe each of the Churches,
'what *Proportion* they may allow out of their 𝔈van-
'gelical 𝔗reaſury, towards the Support of ſuch a
'noble undertaking.

IV. 'But this 𝔈vangelical 𝔗reaſury may be ca-
'pable of being applied unto Some other *Pious Uſes ;*
'and

H 3

' and particularly, unto such as any *Particular Church*
' may See cause to Pursue, for the Service of Religion,
' within their own Vicinity.   Such as, The sending of
' *Bibles*, and *Catechisms*, and other *Instruments of Piety*,
' to be dispersed among the Poor, where it may be
' thought necessary.   Moreover, the Help of New
' Congregations abroad, in their First Essayes, to
' build *Meeting Houses* for the Publick Worship of God
' with Scriptural Purity ; may be one Article of Ex-
' pence for this 𝕰𝖛𝖆𝖓𝖌𝖊𝖑𝖎𝖈𝖆𝖑 𝕿𝖗𝖊𝖆𝖘𝖚𝖗𝖞.

  Quære.   Our Churches have their *Sacramental
Collections.*   Tis not fit indeed, that they should be
without them.   The Primitive Christians had so.
Justin Martyr tells us of the τα συλλεγομενα ; *Tertullian*
Speaks of the, *Deposita Pietatis,* on these occasions.
May not our Churches do well to augment their Liberality, in their Grateful and Joyful *Collections* at the
Table of the Lord, and Resolve, That what is now
Collected, shall be part of their 𝕰𝖛𝖆𝖓𝖌𝖊𝖑𝖎𝖈𝖆𝖑 𝕿𝖗𝖊𝖆𝖘𝖚𝖗𝖞 ; not only, for their Supply of the *Table,* and for
the Relief of the *Poor,* but also for such *Other Services*
to the Kingdom of God, as they may from time to
time, see cause to countenance ?

§. 17.   FRom *Ecclesiastical* Circumstances,
        which in such a Subject as we are
now upon, may with Good Heraldry claim the
Precedency, we will make a Transition to *Political.*
Now, *Touch the Mountains, and they will Smoke !*
Oh ! When will *Wisdom* Visit *Princes* and *Nobles,*
and all the *Judges of the Earth* ; and inspire them
to preserve the due Lustre of their Character, by
a Desire to *Do Good in the Earth* ; a Study to
Glorify the God of Heaven !   The Opportunities
                                        that

that 𝕽𝖚𝖑𝖊𝖗𝖘 have to *Do Good*, are ſo Evident, ſo Numerous, and they have ſo much *Power to Do Good*, that he who addreſſes them, cannot but be overwhelmed with ſome Confuſion of Thought, where to Begin, or when to Conclude, or How to aſſign a fit Order unto them. Indeed the very Definition of Government, is, *A care of other Peoples Safety*. Sirs, From whom have you Received this *Power* ? You could have *no Power at all, Except it were given you from Above.* Certainly what is thus *Receiv'd* from God, ſhould be *Employ'd* for God. *Be wiſe now therefore,* O ye Rulers, *be inſtructed, ye Judges of the Earth. Serve the Lord, with Fear,* leſt ye Forget and Offend Him, who has made you what you are. *Kiſs the Feet of the Son of God, leſt He be Diſpleas'd* at your Neglect of your Duty. Don't *Kindle the Wrath* of Him who is, *The Bleſſed and only Poten-tate, the King of Kings, and Lord of Lords.* What is the Name of a 𝕸𝖆𝖌𝖎𝖘𝖙𝖗𝖆𝖙𝖊 ? The Name which He that made him, has giv'n him, is ; *The Miniſter of God for Good.* His *Empty Name* will produce a *Cruel Crime*, if he dont Set himſelf to *Do Good*, as far as ever he can Extend his In-fluences. Is he a *Vice-gerent* of *God*, and ſhall he do Nothing for *God* ? Groſs Abſurdity *!* Black Ingratitude *!* Is he one of thoſe whom the word of God coming to them has call'd, *Gods* ? *Gods* who *Do no Good*, are ſtrange *Gods.* Not *Gods*, but another Name, too horrible to be men-tioned belongs unto them : ſhall we ſay, *Gods*

that

that have Mouths but they Speak not : Eyes but they See not : Noses but they Smell not, and Hands but they Handle not ? Government is called, *The Ordinance of God.* As the Adminiſtration of it, is to avoid thoſe *Illegalities,* which will render it no other than a *Violation* of the *Ordinance;* thus it ſhould vigorouſly purſue thoſe noble and bleſſed *Ends* for which it is *Ordained ; The Good of Mankind.* Unworthy of all their other flouriſhing *Titles,* be they what they will, are the *Rulers,* who are not ambitious of that above all ; To be Entitled *Benefactors.* The greateſt Monarch in Chriſtendom ; One that by computation has Fourſcore Millions of Subjects, and he whom the Scripture ſtyles, *The Head over many Countryes,* is in the Sacred Prophecies called, *A Vile Perſon.* Verily, ſo is every *Magiſtrate ;* who does not aim to *Do Good in the World. Rulers* who make no other uſe of their Higher Station, than to Swagger over their Neighbours, and command their Obſequious Flatteries, and Enrich themſelves with the Spoils of which they are able to Pillage them, and then wallow in Senſual and Brutal Pleaſures ; Theſe are, *The Baſeſt of Men.* From a ſenſe of this, the *Venetians* tho' they allow Concubines, yet if a man be Obſervably and Exorbitantly given to Senſual Pleaſures, that wiſe People never Employ him : as believing ſuch men to be meer *Good-for-nothings.* Becauſe a Wretched World will continue Indiſpoſed unto the Kingdom of the glorious and only Saviour,
　　　　　　　　　　　　　　　　　　and

and fay, of our *Immanuel, We will not have this Man to Reign over us* ; it is therefore very much put over into the Hands of fuch Selfifh, and Senfual and Wicked *Rulers* : and very -----*centaures.* While the deferved *Curfe* of God remains upon an Impious, and Befotted World, there muft be few *Rulers* that will Serioufly and Strenuoufly *Devife Good,* and Seek to be *Bleffings* unto it. *Rulers* muft, alas, how often be men, whofe *Lives* are not worth a *Prayer,* nor their *Deaths* worth a *Tear.* *Athanafius,* has well anfwered the Queftion, whence 'tis that fuch worthlefs and wicked men get into Authority ? He fays, 'Tis, Διὰ τὸ Εἶναι τὸν λαὸν πονηρόν. *The People are Wicked and muft be Punifhed with men after their own Hearts :---* Thus, when a *Phocas* was made Emperour, a Religious man complained unto Heaven, *Cur fecifti Eum Imperatorem ?* Heaven gave to the complaint that Anfwer, *Non inveni pejorem.* Evil Rulers are well reckon'd by the Hiftorian, among the Effects *Divinæ Ultionis* ; They may go into the catalogue with *Sword,* and *Plague,* and *Fire.* One man may be worfe than All Three. Such bring up the Rear, in the Train of the *Pale Horfe : The Beafts of the Earth.*

O our God, our God, When will thy Compaffions to a Miferable World, appear in beftowing upon it Good Rulers, Able Men, fuch as Fear God, Men of Truth, hating Covetoufnefs ? Oh ! That the Time were come, when there fhall be a Ruler over men, the Juft One, thy JESUS, *Ruling in the Fear of God, and He fhall be as the Light of the Morning,*

ing, when the Sun riseth ; And under Him, the Mountains shall bring Peace to the People, and the Little Hills by Righteousness ; And He will according to His Word make our Officers Peace, and our Exactors Righteousness. Hasten it, in thy Time, O Lord ; But, How long, O Lord, Holy and True, dost thou not Judge ! And make the Kingdoms of this World, thy own, and Remove them that corrupt the Earth ; and in a Great Chain bind up him, who pretends that the Kingdoms of the World are his, and those who are the Rulers of the Darkness of this World !

O All you that Love God, add your *Amen*, to *hasten the Coming of this Day of God !*

In the mean time ;

It cannot be Expreſſed, How much *Good* may be done, by a *Chief Magiſtrate* of a Country, who will make the *Doing of Good,* his *Chief Intention* : A *Conſtantine,* or a *Theodoſius,* or a *Gratian.* The Firſt of theſe, notwithſtanding the vaſt cares of the Empire to take up his Time, yet would every Day at Stated Hours, Retire into his Cloſet & on his *Knees* offer up his *Prayers* unto the glorious GOD. But then, that he might Recommend this Duty unto the World ; this admirable Emperour cauſed his *Image* in all his *Gold Coins,* and his *Pictures* and *Statues,* to be made in a *Praying Poſture,* with his *Hands* Extended, and his *Eyes* lifted up, to Heaven. O *Imperial Piety* ! To behold ſuch a Prince at the Head of it, one would think, were enough to *Convert a World* ! It would, if it were not for the dreadful Energies of one, who is by the *Wrath* of God become, *The Prince of this World* ! I Say, The

The Vertuous *Exemple* of such an One, is almoft enough to Reform whole Nations! It carries irrefiftible *Charms* with it, by which *Totus Componitur Orbis.* A *Prince* Exemplary for Piety, Sheds the Rayes of Heaven, as the *Sun shining* in his Meridian *Strength,* with a moft Penetrating Force into the People, *Rejoycing under his Wings.* Tis now a Rarity ; but it will not be fo, in the Approaching Age, when the *Kings of the Earth, shall bring their Glory and Honour* into the Holy City ! A *Little Piety* in Princes, makes a glaring Show ; The Eyes of their Subjects are Dazzled, their Minds Ravifh'd, with it : They *Numinize* them. What would be done by a *Degree* of *Piety* in them, that fhould bear Proportion to the *Degree* of their *Quality ;* and if their *Piety* were as much above that of other men, as their *Station ?* Roll about, O *Age,* that fhall bring on fuch admirable *Spectacles* !

Tis a vaft Influence that fuch might have on the *Reformation* of the World, and by confequence on its *Felicity,* by difpenfing *Preferments* and *Employments* to none but fuch as may by vertue be recommended unto them. If Good men generally were put into *Commissions,* and none but Good men made *Commanders* at *Sea,* and on *Shore,* what a mighty *Change for the better* would the World immediately be blefs'd withal ! I will beg Leave to fay, It will be a moft comprehenfive Service unto a Nation, to get them unfettered from any *Test,* that may render Honeft

and

and Faithful men, uncapable of Serving them.
And, I will take leave alfo to fay ; The *Dif-placing of a Few Officers* on the Score of their
being found *Vicious Men*, would fignify an hun-dred times as much to Mend the State of a De-praved, Betray'd, unprofperous Nation, as a
Thoufand *Proclamations againft Vice* follow'd with
no fuch Executions.

Good Lawes are important *Machines*, to keep
very much *Evil* out of the World ; yea, they
Reach none, without the *Doing of Some Good* unto
them. All that have any Share in the *Legifla-tive Power*, ought very much to be concerned,
that fuch *Good Lawes* may be Enacted as may be
for a lafting Benefit. The *Reprefentatives* of a
People, in their *Parliaments*, or *Affemblies*, will do
well, to think, *What is there ftill defective in our
Lawes, Leaving the Iniquities or Neceffities of Men
yet not provided againft.* And, *What further Laws
may be propounded, that the Reign of Holineß and
Righteoufnefs may be advanced.* There have been
Lawes, (and fometimes none of the beft, but
Mifchiefs Eftablifhed by Lawes !) which have made
the *Names* of thofe that firft moved for them to be
Remembred. The Remembrance of having
been, *The man that firft moved a Good Law*, were
better than a Statue erected for ones Memory.
But if other men Forget it, Sirs, you will not
want a Recompence in Gods, and your own
Remembrance of it. You know whofe Prayer
it was, *Think upon me, my God, for Good, according
to all that I have done for this People !* Ma-

Magiſtrates may do an unknown Deal of Good, by countenancing of worthy *Miniſters.* To *Settle* and *Support* ſuch *Men of God* in a Place, is to be, as one may ſay, the *Grand-fathers* of all the *Good* which thoſe Men ſhall do in the Place. Their *Conſultations,* and their *Combinations,* with Able, Faithful, Zealous *Miniſters,* may produce more Good Effects than ever any Aſtrology foretold of the moſt happy *Conjunction.* When *Moſes* and *Aaron* joyn to *Do Good,* what can't they do? Queen *Elizabeth* admired the Happineſs of *Suffolk,* in her Progreſs, where ſhe ſaw a mighty good underſtanding between Vertuous *Magiſtrates* and Faithful *Miniſters.*

Briefly. We will obſerve a *Decorum* in our PROPOSALS, and not Suppoſe *Unattentiveneſs* or *Incapacity* in thoſe to whom we offer them. It ſhall only be propoſed, That ſince MAGISTRATES are uſually *Men of Abilities,* they would Retire ſometimes to a Contemplation on that Generous Point, *What Good may I do in the World?* And obſerve, what they are *Able themſelves,* (aſſiſted by the Implored Grace of Heaven,) to *Find out,* as part of the *Good,* which they are to do in *Serving their Generation.*

I forget my ſelf, if old *Theognis* had not a Maxim, which muſt not be Forgotten. *When the Adminiſtration of Affairs, is placed in the Hands of Men, Proud of Command, and bent to their own private Gain, be ſure the People will ſoon be a miſereble People.* I propoſe that the Maxim ſhould
be

be Remembred, and this Mifchief avoided

And this one thing more, *Thinkeft thou this, O man that Judgeft, That thou fhalt efcape the Judgment of God ?* Let the *Judges* of the People, confider, That God will one Day bring them into Judgment.--- *Judex nuper eram ; jam Judicor.* Oh! That *Rulers* would *Realize* to themfelves, as *Real* a matter as any in the World *!* That they muft give an *Account* unto God, concerning their Adminiftration of their *Government.* Sirs, The Great GOD, before whom the Biggeft of you all is but as a Worm of the Duft, will Demand an Account of you, *How Faithful you were in the Difcharge of your Office ? What you did for His Kingdom in your Office ? Whether you did what you could, that the World might be the better for you ?* If you would often take this awful matter in your Confideration, which, Oh ! what *Reafon* you have to do ! ---It could not but Quicken you to very many Actions, which would be *no Grief of Heart* unto you another Day ! He was one of the beft *Rulers,* that ever was in the World, whofe Thoughts run upon that point ; *What fhall I do, when God Rifes up, and when He Vifits, what fhall I anfwer Him ?* Even *Abubeker* the Succeffor of *Mahomet,* upon an Expoftulation with him for his Walking on Foot, when he took a view of his Army, faid, *I fhall find my Account with God for thofe fteps.* He has lefs Chriftianity than a *Mahometan,* who is utterly unmindful of *The Account* he muft give to God, of the fteps taken by him.

How

How well did things go at *Neo-Cæsarea,* when *Basil,* who Liv'd there, could give that Account, concerning the Governour of the Place ! 'That ' he was a moft Exact Obferver of *Juftice;* but ' very *Courteous,* and *Obliging,* and *Eafy of Accefs* ' to the Oppreffed : He was equally at Liefure ' for the *Rich* and for the *Poor ;* But all *Wicked* ' *People* were Afraid of him : He Abhorred Ex- ' ceedingly the taking of a *Bribe* : And his De- ' fign, in fhort, was to raife *Chriftianity* unto its ' Priftine *Dignity.* A *Mahometan* Captain Gene- ral, whofe Name was *Caled,* faid once unto a Chriftian ; *It does not at all become men in eminent Station, to deal Deceitfully and ufe Tricks.* It is a miferable thing, when a *Chriftian* in *Eminent Station,* will do fuch things !

§. 18. THE 𝔓𝔥𝔶𝔰𝔦𝔠𝔦𝔞𝔫 [who fometimes comes alfo to be a *Magiftrate ;* and *Ariftotle* has a Saying very contrary to the *Jewifh* Maxim, That *a City will be happy under fuch a Go- vernment* !] he alfo has his Opportunities to *Do Good,* and render himfelf, *A Beloved Phyfician,* which he is to be advifed of.

Zaccuth the *Portuguefe,* who among many other Books written by him, wrote, *An Hiftory of the principal Phyficians,* was one, who after he had got into *Amfterdam,* did by *Circumcifion* render it Evident, that he had until then, and for Thirty years together, only *Diffembled Chriftianity* at *Lisbon ;* yet becaufe he was very *Charitable* to Poor

Poor Patients, he was very much Esteemed. We now apply our selves to those, whose *Love* to Christianity, we hope, is *without Dissimulation.* There is to be Expected from them, a *Charity* and an *Usefulness*, which may entitle them to a Remembrance in a better *History* than that of *Zacutus Lusitanus* ; yea, in that *Book of Life*, where a Name will be of more account, than to be found in the *Vitæ Illustrium Medicorum*, where *Peter Castellanus* has Embalmed so many of that Profession.

By Serious and Shining *Piety* in your own *Example*, you will bear a glorious Testimony to the *Cause of God and Religion.* You will Glorify the *God of Nature*, and the only Saviour. Your Acquaintance with *Nature*, will indeed be your condemnation, if you do it not. Nothing so *Unnatural* as to be *Irreligious In Religio Medici*, has the Least Reason of any under Heaven, to be an, *Irreligion.* It has been most unreasonably done of them, who have administred occasion, and for that complaint of *Christians* ; *Ubi tres Medici, tres Athei.* It is very sad, That when we read about, the State of the *Rephaim* in the other World, the *Physicians* are by so many Translators, (they think, with too much cause,) carried into it. Very sad, That the *Jews* imagine they have had cause to say, *Optimus inter Medicos ad Gehennam :* and assign this Cause for so severe a Sentence ; *Non enim metuit a Morbis ; Vescitur Laute, nec Confringit cor Suum Deo ; Aliquando Etiam*

Etiam interficit Homines, quando Pauperes, quos Posset, non Sanat. A Sad Story, if it be True!

Sirs ; You will never count your felves to be fuch *Adeptifts*, as to be *at a Stand* in your Studies, and make no further Progrefs in your Enquiries, into *Maladies*,& after *Medicines*. A *Phyfician come to his full growth*, Looks Dangeroufly & Ominoufly. Had the World gone on, with nothing but an *Æfculapius*, furnifhed with a *Goat* (whofe *Milk* for *Pharmacy*) and a *Dog* (whofe *Tongue* for *Cheirurgery*,) we had been miferably of it. You will be Diligent, and Studious, and Inquifitive ; and ftill, *Read* much, and *Think* more, and *Pray* moft of all; and be Sollicitous, to *Find out*, and *Give out*, Something very confiderable for the *Good of Mankind*, which none before you has Lit upon : Be Sollicitous to make fome Addition to the Treafures of your Noble Profeffion. Tho' to attain the Honour of being a *Sydenham*, ---- *Non cuivis homini contingit* ; However, *To Do Something*, may be a Laudable Ambition.

By the Benefit they expect from you, and by the charms of your Polite Education and Proper and Prudent Converfation, You are fometimes Introduced into the *Familiar Acquaintance* of *Great Men*. Perfons of the Firft Quality Entertain you, with much Freedom, and Friendfhip, and Familiarity. Perhaps, you become, under *Hippocrates's* Oath, almoft a Sort of *Confeffors* unto them : as indeed, the *Confeffors* were ufually the *Phyficians* of the People, for feveral Ages.

I

What

What an Advantage to *Do Good,* have you in your Hands, by this Acquaintance ?   The Poor *Jews* both in the *Eastern* and in the *Western* parts of the World, have many a time, had very *Good Offices* done for their Nation, by means of their Country-men arriving to be, *Physicians in ordinary,* unto the *Princes* of the Countries where they have been difperfed.   Sirs, Your Admiffion to feel the Pulfe of *Eminent Perfons,* may Enable you, to do many *Good Offices* for many *Good Interefts.*   You are Perfons of that *Acumen,* that you need not be told, *What* !   You will foon difcover Excellent Things and Ways, wherein *Good* may be done, if you will pleafe to deliberate upon it ; *What Good Motions may I make to my Patient, that he may do Good in the World?*   If you Read what *Gregory Nazianzen* writes of his Brother *Cæsarius,* a famous Phyfician, and a man of Honour, you will doubtlefs find your Difpofitions this way Enkindled.   You know, how ready the *Sick* are, to hear *Good Motions ;*   and how feafonable it is to Ply them therewith, when a Begun *Recovery* from Sickness, befpeaks their Gratitude unto the *God of their Health.*   Yea, & for them that are in Health alfo, you may find, *Molliffima Tempora fandi.*

Physicians often are *Men Univerfally Learned.* They have *Treafure* enough, and fometimes *Liefure* enough, to Write BOOKS, on a vaft Variety of Subjects, whereby *Knowledge* and *Vertue* may be greatly advanced in the World.   The late *Epick Poems* of a *Blackmore,* & *Cofmologia Sacra*
of

of a *Grew*, are fresh Examples ; Mankind is indebted unto those Learned Physicians ; the Names of the *Hero's* are immortalized ; they need no *Statues* : nor need they mind the Envy of any Modern *Theophrastus.* A *Catalogue* of BOOKS Written, on various Arguments, besides those of their own Profession, (and unto better Purpose too, than only to Produce *Erastianism* in the Churches which our Glorious Lord has instituted) by *Learned Physicians,* would it self alone almost make a *Book.* In the *Great Army* of *Learned Physicians,* that have *Published* their Labours about the *Word which the Lord has given,* and for the Service of His Church, and World, I humbly move, that the Incomparable *Zuinger,* and *Gesner* may appear as *Field-Officers.* A City *Tauris* were too mean a Present, for *Physicians* of such merits. I propose them to Imitation ; that many may *Follow such Leaders.* You know, *Freher* has brought on his *Theatre,* near Five Hundred famous *Physicians,* with some Account of their *Lives* and *Works* ; very few *Britons* among them ; and none at all that Lived unto the End of the former Century. What a vast Addition might there be since made unto that *List of Honour* from the *British* Nations ! May an Excellent Ambition to be part of it, Excite the Capable, to *Do Worthily* !

Physicians are even over-stock'd with Opportunities, to help the *Poor,* and heal them for Nothing. It was a Noble saying of *Cicero, Nil habet Fortuna melius, quam ut possis, neque Natura Præstan-*

tius, quam ut velis, fervare Plures. But **I** will fet
before you an higher confideration, than what
a Pagan *Kirker* was ever acquainted with. Sirs,
The more Charity, and Compaffion, and Con-
defcenfion you treat the *Poor* withal, the more
will you arrive to, *The Greateft of all Glories :* I fay,
The *Greateft* & *Higheft* of all Glories ! --- I mean,
An Imitation of your Admirable SAVIOUR.
You will readily fay, *Quod decuit CHRISTUM,
cur mibi Turpe putem ?* In comparifon of this
Confolation, it will be a fmall Thing to fay unto
you, That your coming among the *Poor,* will be
like the Defcent of the Angel of *Betbefda* unto
them. We will not prefume to prefcribe unto
you, What *Good* you fhall Do to the *Poor,* and by
what Generous Actions you fhall *Take their Infirmities and bear their Sickneffes.* Only we Enter
an Objection againft your taking any *Fees* for
your *Vifits* on the *Lords-Day*'s, Becaufe, the *Time*
is none of *Yours* ; 'Tis the *Lords* !

When we Confider how much the *Lives* of
Men are in the *Hands* of God ; and what a De-
pendence we have on the *God of our Health* for
our Cure, when we have loft it ; and what
Strange and Strong *Proofs* we have had, of *Angels*
by their Communications or Operations Con-
tributing to the Cure of the Difeafes where-with
Mortals have been Oppreffed ; [whereof I can
my felf relate aftonifhing Inftances !] and the
Marvellous Efficacy of *Prayer* for the Recovery
of a *Sick Brother, who bas not Sinn'd a Sin unto Death ;*
                                                    What

What better thing is there to be recommended unto a *Phyſician,* who deſires to *Do Good,* than this ; *Good Sir, Be a Man of Prayer.* In your Daily and Secret *Prayer* carry every one of your *Patients* by Name, (as you would your own Children,) unto the Glorious *Lord our Healer,* for His Healing *Mercies* : Place them as far as your *Prayer* will do it, under the *Beams* of the *Sun of Righteouſneſſ.* And as any *New Caſe* of your Patients may occur, eſpecially if there be any Difficulty in it, why ſhould you not make your Particular and Sollicitous Applications to Heaven for Direction ! *O Lord, I know that the way of man is not in himſelf, nor is it in man that walketh, to direct his Steps ;* No, nor in man that healeth, to perform his Cures. *Hippocrates* adviſed Phyſicians, that when they Viſited their Patients, they ſhould conſider, whether there might not be, *Divinum quiddam in morbo.* Truly, in ſome ſenſe, there is ever ſo, and it ſhould be conſidered. What an *Heavenly Life* might you lead, if your Buſineſs may be carried on with as many Viſits to *Heaven,* as you make unto your *Patients* ! One *Jacob Tzaphalon,* a famous Jew in the former Century, Publiſhed at *Venice,* a Book Entituled, *Precious Stones.* There are ſeveral *Prayers* in the Book ; and among them a Pretty long one, *For Phyſicians when they go to Viſit their Patients.* When the Pſalmiſt ſayes, *Thou haſt made me wiſer than my Enemies ;* it may be read, *Thou haſt made me wiſe from my Enemies.* We ſhould Learn *Wiſ-*

dom from them; *Fas eft, et ab hofte !--- O Chriftianity*, certainly thou wilt Out-do *Judaifm* in thy Devotions !

We read, *Heavinefs in the Heart of Man makes it Stoup, but a Good Word makes it Glad.* We read, *A Cheerful Heart doth Good like a Medicine, but a broken Spirit drieth the Bones.* And *Baglivi* is not the only Phyfician, who has made the Obfervation, 'That a great part of our 'Difeafes, either do Rife from, or are Fed by, a '*Weight of Cares* lying on the *Minds* of Men. Difeafes 'that feem *Incureable*, are Eafily cured by Agreeable 'Converfation, *Diforders* of the *Mind*, firft bring Dif-'eafes on the *Stomach* ; and fo the whole Mafs of 'Blood gradually becomes infected. And as long as the '*Paffions* of the *Mind* continue, the *Difeafes* may indeed 'change their *Forms*, but they rarely quit the Patients. *Tranquillity of Mind* will do Strange Things, towards the Relief of *Bodily Maladies.* Tis not without Reafon, that *Hofman*, in his Differtation, *Des Moyens de vivre longtems*, does infift on *Tranquillity of Mind* as the chief among the *Wayes to Live Long* ; and that this is the caufe why we read, *The Fear of the Lord tendeth to Life.* They that have Practifed, *The Art of Curing by Expectation*, have made an Experiment of what the *Mind* will do towards the Cure of the *Body.* By Practifing, *The Art of Curing by Confolation*, you may carry on the Experiment. I Propound then, Let the *Phyfician* with all poffible Ingenuity of *Converfation*, find out, what matter of *Anxiety*, there may have been upon the Mind of his *Patient* ; what there is, that has made his Life *Uneafy* to him. Having Difcovered the *Burden*, Let him ufe all the wayes he can devife to take it off. Offer him fuch *Thoughts*, as may be the beft *Anodynes* for his Diftreffed Mind ; Efpecially, the *Right Thoughts of the Righteous*, and the wayes to a compofure upon

Re-

Religious Principles. Give him a *Prospect*, if you can, of some *Deliverance* from his Diftreffes, or some *Abatement* of them. Raife in him as *Bright Thoughts* as may be, and Scatter the *Clouds*, remove the *Loads*, which his Mind is Perplexed withal: Efpecially, by Reprefenting & Magnifying the *Mercy* of GOD in CHRIST unto him. It is Poffible, Sir, That you may in this way alfo, find our *Obliging Occafions* to Exercife abundance of *Goodnefs*, in Doing your felf, or in bringing others to Do, *Kindneffes* for the Miferable.

And what fhould hinder you, from Confidering the *Souls* of your *Patients*, their *Interiour State* ; their *Spiritual Health* ; what they *have done*,& what they *have to do*, that they may be in *Good Terms with Heaven*? You may from their *Natural Diftempers*,affect your own Minds,& theirs too, with a Senfe of our *Analogous Moral* ones. You may make your Converfation with them, a *Vehicle* for fuch *Admonitions of Piety* as may be moft *Needful* for them: That they may neither be found *Unprepared* for *Death*, nor *Unthankful* & *Unfruitful* upon their efcaping of it. This you may do, without any Indecent Intrufion into the Office of the *Minifter*; But you may indeed at the fame Time do many a Good Office for the *Minifter*, as well as for the *Patient*, and inform the Minifter when and where and how he may be very Serviceable among fome of the Miferable, with whofe condition he may elfe happen to be unacquainted. The *Art of Healing* was, you know, firft brought into order by men that had the *Care of Souls*. And I know not why they who profefs and practife that Noble *Art*, fhould now wholly caft off that *Care*! Perhaps you Remember a *King*, who was alfo a *Phyfician* [For other *Crowned Heads*, befides *Mithridates* and *Hadrianus* and *Conftantinus Pogonatus*, have been fo !] and who gave this Reafon why the *Greeks* had fuch Difeafes among them fo much uncured; *Becaufe they neglected their Souls, the*

chief

chief thing of all. For my part, I know not why the *Phyfician* fhould wholly *negleɛt the Souls* of his Patients! I will hold you no Longer. You are not ignoranr, that *Medicine* in the World, once was, and in many Ungofpellized parts of the World ftill is, *A Thing horribly Magical. Celfus* tells it, as a part of the *Egyptian Philofophy* current in his Time, That the Body of man is divided into *Thirty Six* Parts, each of which was the peculiar Allotment and Poffeffion of a *Dæmon* ; and this *Dæmon* was by the *Magi* call'd upon, to cure Difeafes of the part that belong'd unto him. Even in *Galens* time we find *Preftigiaturas Ægyptias* Practifed ; he himfelf writes of them. Other Countries were from *Ægypt* infected with them. Hence *Medicines* were called, *Pharmaca* The *Oriental* Nations had their *Teraphim* for the cure of Difeafes. Whence Θεραπευω fignifies, both to *Worfhip,* and to *Cure.* And, *Curæ Morborum,* is reckoned by *Eufebius* one main Article of the *Pagan Theology.* God ufed all proper Means, for Saving His People, from having to do with that fort of *Men,* or of *Means.* He Commended unto them, the Study of Nature, and of Natural Remedies. They did after the Example of *Solomon,* Study *Botanicks* : They had their *Apothecaries* who were to furnifh them with *Materials* for Medicines. The Princes of *Judea* had, as *Pliny* tells us, Their *Phyfick Gardens.* Probably *Naboths* Vineyard might have fuch an one in it ; which might be the Reafon why *Ahab* did fo Covet it. And *Joram,* the Son of *Ahab,* repaired hither, to be cured of his Wounds. An Excellent Phyfician, in a late Compofition with which he has obliged the Publick, thinks, The Sin of *Afa,* when he *Sought not unto the Lord, but unto the Phyficians,* was, both occafioned and Aggravated by this ; There were at this time none but *Magical Phyficians.* But fome others have thought, that fome of *Afa's* Anceftors had been

Medically

Medically difpofed, and were Students in the *Art of Healing.* From hence might come the Name of *Afa* : for *afa* is the *Chaldee* word for a *Phyfician.* It may be, for that caufe thisKing might have the Greater Efteem for thofe who were skill'd in *Medicines,* and put a *Confidence* in them, that had with it and in it, a Negle&t of the glorious GOD ; the only Author and Giver of Health. What I aim at, in this Paragraph, is but Summarily to befpeak the *Reverfe* of all this; That my Honourable *Afa,* [*Honourable!* the Son of *Sirach* has taught me to call him fo !] would himfelf continually go to *God our Saviour* on all occafions, and as far as he can, bring all his *Patients* thither alfo.

Finally ; An Induftrious and an Ingenious Gentleman of your Profeffion, has a Paffage in a Preface to his, *Pharmacopæia Bateana,* which, I will here infert : becaufe very many of you can Speak the like ; and by inferting it, I propofe, to increafe the Number.

'I know no poor Creature that Ever came to me
'in my whole Time, that once went from me, with-
'out my Defired Help *gratis.* And I have accounted
'the Reftoration of fuch a Poor and Wretched Crea-
'ture, a greater Bleffing to me, than if I had gotten
'the Wealth of both the *Indies.* I can't fo well Ex-
'prefs my felf concerning this matter, as I can conceive
'it ; but I am fure, I fhould have been more pleafed,
'and had a greater Satisfa&tion, in feeing fuch an
'Helplefs creature Reftored to its Defired Health,than
'if I had found a very valuable Treafure. All the
'Good I have done in thefe cafes, as I never can Re-
'pent it, fo I Refolve to continue it ; For I certainly
'know, I have had the Signal Bleffing of God, at-
'tending my Endeavours, for it.

§. 19.

§. 19. *I Will get me unto the Rich Men, ---- and will Speak unto them :* For they will *know the wayes* to *Do Good,* and will think, what they shall be able to say, when they come into the *Judgment of their God.* An English Person of Quality, quoting that Passage, *The Desire of a Man is his Kindness,* invited me so to read it, *The* only *Desireable thing in a man is his Goodness.* How Happy would the World be if every Person of Quality would come into this Perswasion ! It is an Article in my Commission ; *Charge them that are Rich in this World, That they Do Good, that they be Rich in Good Works, Ready to Distribute, willing to Communicate.* In pursuance thereof, I will put *Rich Men* in mind of the Opportunities to *Do Good,* with which the God, who *gives Power to Get Wealth,* has favoured and obliged and enriched them. It was an Account, and a very Good one it was, that has been sometimes given of a Good man ; *The Wealth of this World, he knew no Good in it, but the doing of Good with it.* Yea, those men who have had very little *Goodness* in them, yet in describing, *The manners of the Age,* in which they have had perhaps themselves too deep a Share, have seen cause to Subscribe and Publish this prime Dictate of Reason ; *We are never the better for any thing, barely for the Propriety Sake ; but it is the Application of it, that gives every thing its value. Whoever buries his Talent, breaks a Sacred Trust, and Cozens those that Stand*

in

in need on't. Sirs, You cannot but Acknowledge, That it is the Sovereign GOD, who has bestow'd upon you, the *Riches* which distinguish you. A *Devil* himself, when he Saw a *Rich Man*, could not but make this Acknowledgment unto the God of Heaven, *Thou haft Blessed the work of his hands, and his Substance is increased in the Land.* It is also a Thing, whereof 'tis to be hoped, you are not unapprehensive, That the *Riches* in your possession are some of the *Talents*, whereof you must give an Account unto the Glorious LORD, who has betrusted you therewithal : And that you will *give up your Account with Grief, and not with Joy*, if it must be found, that *All* your Estates have been laid out, only to gratify the Appetites of the *Flesh*, and *Little* or *Nothing* of them consecrated unto the Service of *God*, and of His Kingdom in the World. We read of the Servants assign'd unto the *Priests* of old, *Unto you they are given as a Gift for the Lord.* It is what is to be said of all our *Estates.* What God gives us, is not given us for our selves, but *for the Lord.* And, *Cum crescunt Dona crescunt etiam Rationes Donorum.* Indeed there is hardly any Professor of Christianity, so *Vitious*, but he will own, that All of his Estate is to be used in *Honest Uses* ; and part of it, in *Pious Uses.* If any plead their *Poverty*, to Excuse them, and Exempt them, from doing any thing this way, O *Poor Widow* with thy *two Mites*, Eternized in the History of the Gospel, Thou shalt *Rise up in the Judgment with*
that

that Generation, and (halt Condemn them. And let them alſo know, that they take a courſe, to condemn and confine themſelves unto Eternal *Poverty.* But the main Queſtion is, about the *Quota Parts;* How much of a Mans Income is to be Devoted unto *PiousUſes?* And now, Let it not ſeem an *Hard Saying,* if I ſay unto you, That a *Tenth Part* is the leaſt that you can bring under a more *Solemn Dedication* unto the Lord ; for whom indeed,after ſome ſort, we are to lay out our *All.* A Farthing leſs, would make an Enlightened and Conſiderate Chriſtian, Suſpicious, of his coming under the Danger of a *Sacriledge.* By the *Pious Uſes* for which your *Tenths* are thus challenged, I do not intend only the *Maintenance of the Evangelical Miniſtry,* but alſo the Relief of the *Miſerable* whom our Merciful Saviour has made the Receivers of His Rents, and all that is to be more direЄly done, for the Preſerving and Promoting of *Piety* in the World. Since there is a *Part* of every mans Revenues due to the Glorious Lord, and ſuch *Pious Uſes,* it is not Fit that the Determination of *What Part,* it muſt be, ſhould be left unto ſuch Hearts as ours. My Friend Thou haſt, it may be,too high an Opinion of thy own *Wiſdom* and *Goodneſs,* if nothing but thy own *Carnal Heart,* ſhall determine ſtill *When,* and *What,* thy Revenues are to do, for Him, whom thou art ſo ready to *Forget,* when He has *Filled* thee. But if the LORD Himſelf, to whom thou art but a *Steward,* has
fixed

fixed any part of our ufual *Revenues,* for Himfelf, as 'tis moft Reafonable that He fhould have the Fixing of it, certainly a *Tenth* will be found the leaft that He has called for. A *Tenth* is the *Leaft Part* in the Firft Divifion of Numbers, which is that of *Unites.* *Grotius* notes it, as the Foundation for the Law of Tithes ; *Numerus Denarius Gentibus ferme cunctis Numerandi Finis eft.* It is but fair, and the very *Light of Nature* will declare for it ; That the Great GOD, who with a *Seventh Day,* is own'd as the *Creator,* fhould with a *Tenth* part be own'd as the *Poffeffor* of All Things. We don't Allow Him fo much as *The Leaft,* if we withold a *Tenth* from Him. Lefs than *That,* is lefs than what all Nations make *The Leaft.* Certainly, To withold this, is to *Withold more than is Meet.* Sirs, you know the *Tendency.* Long before the *Mofaick* Difpenfation of the Law, we find, that this was *Jacobs* Vow, *The Lord fhall be my God, and of all that thou fhalt give me, I will furely give the Tenth unto thee.* It feems we do not fufficiently Declare, *That the Lord is our God,* if we do not *Give a Tenth* unto Him. And how can we approve our felves *Ifraelites Indeed,* if we fleight fuch a Pattern of our *Father Jacob ?* I will afcend a Little Higher. In one Text we read of our *Father Abraham, He gave Melchizedek the Tenth of all.* In another Text we read of our Saviour JESUS, *Thou art a Prieft for ever after the Order of Melchizedek.* Hence I form this Argument ; The Rights of *Melchizedek* belong to our
JESUS,

JESUS, the *Royal High-Priest* now concerned in the Heavens for us.   The *Tenths* were the Right of *Melchizedek.*   Therefore the *Tenths* belong to our JESUS.   I do in my Conscience believe, *That this Argument cannot be answered.*   The man seems to blur one Evidence of his being one of the true Children of *Abraham,* that goes to answer it I do Renew my *Appeal* to the *Light of Nature. To Nature thou shalt go!*   'Tis very certain, That the Ancient Pagans did use to *Decimate* for *Sacred Uses. Pliny* tells us, the *Arabians* did so.   *Xenophon* tells us, the *Grecians* did so.   You find the custom, as old as the Pen of *Herodotus* can carry it.   Tis confirmed by *Pausanias,* and by *Diodorus Siculus.*   A whole Army of Authors, besides *Doughty,* have related this, and asserted it.   I will only bring in *Festus,* to Speak for them all : *Decima quæque Veteres Dijs Suis offerebant. Christian,* Wilt thou Do less for thy GOD, than the Poor Perishing *Pagans* did for Theirs?   *Oh! Tell it not!* --- But this I will tell ; That they who have conscientiously Employ'd their *Tenths* in *Pious Uses,* have usually been Blessed in their Estates, with a very Remarkable Providence of God. The Blessing has been sometimes Delay'd, with some Trial of their *Patience : Not for any Injustice in their Hands ;* Their *Prayer* has been *Pure.* And their *Faith* of the *Future State* has been sometimes try'd, by their Meeting with some Losses, and some Disappointments.   But then, their *Little* has been so Bless'd, as to be still a *Competency ;* and

and God has Bleſs'd them with ſo much *Contentation* in it, that it has yielded *more* unto them, than the *much* of many others. And *very often,* I ſay, *very often,* they have been Rewarded with a ſtrange Succeſs, and Increaſe of their Eſtates; even in this World, ſeen the Fulfilment of that Word; *Caſt thy Grain into the moiſt Ground; for thou ſhalt find it after many Dayes.* And that word; *Honour the Lord with thy Subſtance; ſo ſhall thy Barns be filled with* Plenty. Hiſtory has given us many and charming Examples, of thoſe, who have had their Conſcientious *Decimations* Followed & Rewarded with a Surpriſing Proſperity of their Affairs; And ſmall *Mechanicks,* or *Husbandmen,* have Riſen to Eſtates, which once they never durſt have dreamed of. The Excellent *Gouge,* in his Treatiſe Entituled, *The Sureſt and Safeſt way of Thriving,* has collected ſome ſuch Examples. The Jewiſh Proverb, *Decima, ut Dives fias;* or, *Tythe and be Rich!* would be oftner verified, if oftner Practiſed. *Prove me now herewith, faith the Lord of Hoſts, if I will not pour out a Bleſſing upon you!* But let the Demand of *Liberal Things* grow upon you. *A Tenth,* I have called, *The Leaſt.* For ſome, 'tis much *Too Little.* Men of great Eſtates, that would not *Sow for their Fleſh, & reap Corruption,* May and will often go beyond a *Decimation.* Some of them riſe to a *Fifth;* and the Religious Counteſs of *Warwick,* would not ſtop at any thing ſhort of a *Third.* The Gentlemen my Readers, will Excuſe me, if I carry them no

Higher,

Higher, and say nothing to them, of a *Joannes Eleemosynarius*, who annually made a Distribution of all to Pious *Uses;* and having made even with his Revenues, then said, *I bless God that I have now nothing left, but my Lord and Master* CHRIST, *whom I long to be withal, and whom I can with unentangled Wings now fly unto!* Yet I will mention to them the Example of some Eminent Merchants, who have set their Estates at a Moderate and Competent Elevation, and Resolved, They would never be any *Richer* than *That.* They have carried on a Great and Quick Trade ; but what ever *Gain* carried their Estates beyond the *Set Sum*, they Devoted it all to *Pious Uses.* And were any of them, ever *Losers?* Never one of them *!* The Christian Emperour *Tiberius* 2. was *famous* for his Religious Bounties; His Empress thought him even *Profuse*, in them. He told her, *He should never want Money so long as in Obedience to the Command of a Glorious Christ, he did Supply the Necessities of the Poor, and abound in such Religious Bounties.* Once, immediately after he had made a Liberal Distribution, he unexpectedly found a mighty Treasure ; and there were Tidings also brought him, of the Death of a Man vastly Rich, who had bequeathed all his Wealth unto him. Lesser men can tell very many, and very taking Stories of this Importance, even from their own happy Experience. I cannot forbear Transcribing some Lines of my Honoured *Gouge* on this occasion.

'I

' I am verily Perfwaded, that there is Seldom any
' Man, who giveth to the Poor Proportionably to
' what God has beftowed on him, but if he does ob-
' ferve the Paffages of Gods Providence towards him,
' he fhall find the fame Doubled and Redoubled upon
' him in *Temporal Bleffings.* I dare challenge all the
' World, to give one Inftance, (or at leaft any confi-
' derable Number of Inftances) of any *Merciful Man,*
' whofe Charity has undone him. But, as *Living*
' *Wells,* the more they are Drawn, the more freely
' they Spring and Flow ; fo the Subftance of Charita-
' ble Men, does oftentimes Multiply in the very Diftri-
' bution ; Even as the Five Loaves and Few Fifhes
' did multiply in their Breaking and Diftributing ;
' and the Widows Oyl increafed by the pouring it
' out.

I will add a confideration, wherein, methinks,
common *Humanity* fhould be fenfible of a *Provo-*
cation. Let *Rich* Men who are not *Rich towards*
God, efpecially fuch as have no Children of their
own, to make the *Heirs* of their *Hoarded Riches,*
confider the vile Ingratitude, which the
Forks that come after them, will treat them,
withal. Sirs, They will hardly allow you a *Tomb-*
ftone ; And, wallowing in the *Wealth* which you
have left, (but they complain, that you left it
no fooner unto them) they will only play upon
your *Memory,* fquib upon your *Husbandry,* ridicule all your *Parfimony*! How much more *Wif-*
dom, would it be, for you to *Do Good* with your
Eftates while you *Live* ; and at your *Death* do
That, which may Embalm your Name to Pofte-
rity in this World, and be for your Advantage
K   in

in that which you are going unto ! That your *Souls* may *Dwell* in all the *Eafe* and *Good* of the *Paradifian* Reflections, at the Time, when others *Inherit* what you leave unto them.

I only now annex the complement of one to his Friend, upon his Acceffion to an Eftate ; *Much Good may it do you; that is, Much Good may you do with it.*

I hope, we are now Ready for PROPOSALS. We fhall Set our felves, *To Devife Liberal Things.*

Gentlemen, It is of old faid, *Res eft Sacra Mifer.* To *Relieve the Neceffities of the Poor* [*Non Paviftis, occidiftis ;*] this is a thing Acceptable to the Compaffionate God ; who has given to *You,* what He might have given to *Them* ; and has given it unto *You* that you might have the *Honour* and *Pleafure* to Impart it unto *them* : And who has told you, *He that has Pitty on the Poor, Lends unto the Lord.* The more you confider the *Command* and *Image* of a Glorious CHRIST in what you do this way, the more Affurance you have, that in the *Day of God,* you fhall joyfully hear Him Saying, *You have done it unto me!* And the more Humble, Silent, Referved *Modefty* you exprefs, concealing even from the *Left Hand* what is done with the *Right,* the more you are Affured of, *A Great Reward in the Heavenly World.* Such *Liberal* men, 'tis obferved, are ufually *Long-Lived* Men. *Fruftus Liberat Arborem.* And at laft, they pafs from this unto *Everlafting Life.*

The Name of a LADY, what is it in the Original Senfe of the Word ? It was firft, *Leafdian,* then *Lafdy* : from *Leaf,* or *Laf,* which Signifies, *A Loaf of Bread.* And from *D'ian to Serve.* As much as to fay, *One who diftributes Bread.* The true LADY, is one who feeds the *Poor,* and makes agreeable *Diftributions* to their *Indigencies.* In the Dayes of Primitive

Chriftianity, the *Ladies* of the beft Quality, would Seek and Find out the *Sick,* and Vifit the *Hoffitals,* and fee what Help they wanted ; and help them with an admirable Alacrity. The Mother, and the Sifter of *Nazianzen,* what a *Good Report* have they obtained from his Pen,for their unwearied Bounties to the *Poor?* Emprefles themfelves have Stouped, & they never Look'd fo *Great,* as in their Stouping, to releive the Miferable,

··· *And when they Stoup'd, it was to do Some Good to others. Angels, they do fo!*

When you keep your *Dayes* of *Prayers,* now is a Special Seafon for your *Alms :* That your *Prayers* may go up with your *Alms,* as a *Memorial before the Lord.* Verily, There are *Prayers* in *Alms.* And, *Is not this the Faft that I have Chofen,faith the Lord :* The Note of the Beggar among the Jews was, *Deferve Something by me.* Among us, it may be. *Obtain Something by me.*

There is a City in the World, where every Houfe hath a Box hanging in a Chain, on which is Written, *Think on the Poor ;* and they commonly conclude no Bargain, but more or lefs is put into the Box. The *Deacons* have the Key, and once a Quarter go round the City,and take out the Money. When that City was like to have been loft, One who was not the beft man in the World, yet could fay, *That he was of Opinion, God would preferve that City from being Deftroy'd, if it were only for the Great Charity they Exprefs to the Poor.* Tis the RicheftCity of the RicheftCountry,for its Bignefs, that ever was in the World. A City that it is thought, fpends yearly in Charitable Ufes, more than all the Revenues which the whole Fine Country of the Grand Duke of *Tufcany* brings in to the Arbitrary Mafter of it. You know, *Manus Pauperum eft Chrifti Gazophylacium.*

When you Difpenfe your *Alms,* unto the *Poor,* who
K 2   know,

know, what it is to *Pray*, you may oblige them to *Pray* for you by Name every Day. Tis an Excellent Thing to have, *The Blessing of them that have been Ready to Perish, thus coming upon you*. Behold, A Surprising Sense in which you may be, *Praying always*. You are so, even while you are *Sleeping*, if those whom you have so obliged are thus *Praying* for you! And Now, Look for the Accomplishment of that word ; *Blessed* is he that considers the *Poor* ; *The Lord will Preserve him and Keep him Alive* ; *and he shall be blessed on the Earth*.

Very often your *Alms* are dispersed among such as very much need *Admonitions of Piety* to accompany them. Can't you contrive, to intermix a *Spiritual Charity*, with your *Temporal*? Perhaps you may Discourse with them about the *State of their Souls*, and obtain from them, which you now have a Singular Advantage to do, some *Declared Resolutions* to Do what they ought to do. Or else you may convey Little *Books* unto them, which certainly they will Promise to *Read*, when you thus bespeak their doing so.

Charity to the *Souls* of Men, is undoubtedly the Highest and the Noblest *Charity*, and of the greatest Consequence. To furnish the Poor with *Catechisms*, and *Bibles*, is to do an unknown Deal of *Good* unto them: To Publish and Scatter *Books of Piety*, and to put into the Hands of Mankind such *Treatises of Divinity* as may have a Tendency to make them *Wiser* or *Better* ; no man knows what *Good* he does in doing such things ! It was exellently done of some Good men, who, a little while ago were at the Charge of Printing Thirty Thousand of the, *Alarm to the Unconverted*, written by *Joseph Allein*, to be all given away unto such as would promise to Read it. A man of no great Estate has before now with no great Trouble, given away the best part of a Thousand Books *of Piety*, Every year for many years together. Who can tell, but with the Expence

of

of lefs than a Shilling, Sir, you may *Convert a Sinner from the Error of his way, & Save a Soul from Death* ! A worfe Doom, than a, *Damnatio ad metalla,* is upon the *Soul,* who had rather hoard up hisMoney,thanEmploy it on fuch a *Charity.*

He that *Supports the Office* of the *Evangelical Miniftry,* Supports a *Good Work;* and performs One ; yea, at the Second Hand performs what is done by the skilful, faithful, painful Minifter, and that is *many* an one. The Encouraged Servant of the Lord, will do the more *Good,* for your Affiftences, Tis done for a Glorious CHRIST, what you have done for *him* ; and in Confideration of the *Glorious Gofpel* Preached by him. And you fhall *Receive a ProphetsReward*! *Luther* Said,*Si quid Scholafticis confers, Deo ipfi Contulifti.* Tis more Senfibly So, when the *Scholars* are become Godly & Ufeful *Preachers.*

I have read this Paffage, ' It was for feveral years, ' the Practice of a Worthy Gentleman, in Renewing ' his Leafes, inftead of making it a Condition, that his ' Tenants fhould keep an *Hawk* or a *Dog* for him, to ' oblige them, that they fhould keep a *Bible* in their ' Houfes, for themfelves, and fhould bring up their ' Children to *Read* and be *Catechifed.* *Land lords,* 'Tis worth your Confidering, whether you may not in your *Leafes,* infert fome *Claufes,* that may Serve the Kingdom of God. You are his *Tenants,* in thofe very *Freeholds,* where you are *Land lords* to other men ! Oblige your *Tenants* to Worfhip God in their Families.

To take a *Poor Child,* efpecially an *Orphan,* Left in *Poverty,* and beftow an *Education* upon it, efpecially if it be a *Liberal Education,* is an admirable, & a complicated *Charity*; yea, it may draw on a long Train of *Good,* and intereft you in all the *Good* that fhall be done by thofe whom you have Educated.

Hence alfo what is done for *Schools,* and for *Colledges,* and for *Hofpitals,* is done for a *General Good.* The

Endowing of thefe, or the *Maintaining* of them, is, *At once to Do Good unto many.*

But, alas, how much of the *Silver* and *Gold* in the World, is buried in Hands, where 'tis little better than convey'd back to the *Mines* from whence it came? Or Employ'd unto as little purpofe, as what arrives at *Indoftan*, where a large part of the *Silver* and *Gold* of the World, is after a Circulation carried as unto a Fatal Center, and by the *Moguls* lodg'd in Subferraneous Caves, never to fee the light any more. *Talia non facit bonæ Fides ae fpei Chriftianus.*

Sometimes there may be got ready for the Prefs, Elaborate Compofures, of Great *Buik*, and Greater *Worth*, by which the beft Interefts of *Knowledge* and *Vertue*, may be confiderably Served in the World; [Perhaps, what may be called, as the *Oƌapla of Origen* was, *Opus Ecclefiæ* :] they ly like the impotent Man at the Pool of *Bethefda* ; and there they are like to ly, till God infpire Some Wealthy Perfons, to Subfcribe nobly for their Publication, and by this Generous Application of their Wealth to bring them abroad! The *Names* of fuch Noble Benefactors to Mankind, ought to *Live*, as long as the *Works* themfelves ; where the *Works* do any Good, what thefe have done towards the Publifhing of them, *Ought to be told for a Memorial of them.*

Yea, I will carry the matter further than fo. The Saying may feem to carry fome Affront in it ; *Idle Gentlemen and Idle Beggars, are the Pefts of the Common Wealth.* But they that are offended muft quarrel with the Afhes of a Bifhop. T'was Dr. *Sanderfons.* Will you then think, Sirs, of fome Honourable and Agreeable Employments? I will mention one. The *Pythagoreans* forbad mens eating their own Brains ; or keeping their good Thoughts to themfelves. Tis an Obfervation of the Incomparable *Boyl*, ' That as to *Religieus Books* in
' general,

' general, it has been Obferved, That thofe Penn'd
' by *Lay-men*, and efpecially *Gentlemen*, have (*Cæteris*
' *Paribus*) been better Entertained, and more Effectu-
' al than thofe of *Ecclefiafticks*.   We all know, His own
were fo.   It is no rare thing for Men of Quality, to
accomplifh themfelves in *Languages* and *Sciences*, until
they have been Prodigies of Literature.   Their *Li-*
braries too, have been Stupendous Collections ; approaching towards *Vatican* or *Bodlefian* Dimenfions.
An *Englifh Gentleman* has been fometimes the moft
Accomplifh'd Thing in the whole World.   How many of
thefe (befides a *Leigh*, a *Wolfely*, or a *Polhil*,) have been
Benefactors to Mankind by their incomparable Writings ?   It were mightily to be wifh'd, That *Rich*
Men, and Perfons of an Elevated Condition, would
Qualify themfelves, for the ufe of the *Pen*, as well as
of the *Sword* ; and by their *Pen* deferve to have it faid
of them, *They have Written Excellent things*.   An Englifh *Perfon of Quality* in a Book of his Entituled, *A View*
of the Soul, has a Paffage, which I will Addrefs you
with.   Sayes he, *It is certainly, the Higheft Dignity, if*
not the Greateft Happinefs, Humane Nature is capable
of, here in the vale below, to have the Soul fo far enlightned
as to become the Mirror, or Conduit, or Conveyer of Gods
Truth to others.   It is an Ill Motto for Men of Capacity,
𝔐𝔶 𝔘𝔫𝔡𝔢𝔯𝔰𝔱𝔞𝔫𝔡𝔦𝔫𝔤 𝔦𝔰 𝔘𝔫𝔣𝔯𝔲𝔦𝔱𝔣𝔲𝔩.   Gentlemen,
Confider what *Subjects* may moft Properly & Ufefully
fall under your *Cultivation*.   Your *Pen* will Stab *Atheifm*
and *Wickednefs*, with an Efficacy beyond other mens :
If out of your *Tribe* there come thofe who *handle the*
Pen of the Writer, they will do uncommon Execution.
One of them has ingenioufly told you ; *Tho' I know*
fome Functions, yet I know no Truths of Religion, like the
Shew-bread ; Matth. 12. 4 only for the Priefts.

I will addreſs you, with one PROPOSAL more. Tis, That you would [As *Ambroſius* had his *Origen*,] wiſely chuſe a *Friend* of Shining A- bilities, of Hearty Affections, and of Excellent Piety : A *Miniſter* of ſuch a Character, if it may be. And Entreat him, yea, Oblige him, to *Study* for you, and *Suggeſt* to you, *Opportunities to Do Good* : make him, as I may ſay, your *Monitor*. Let him Adviſe you from time to time, what *Good* you may do. Cauſe him to ſee, that he never gratifies you more, than by his Advice upon this Intention. If a *David* have a *Seer* to do ſuch a Good Office for him, and be on the *Look out* for to find out what Good he may do, what Services may be done for the *Temple* of God in the World !

There ſeems no Need of adding any thing but this. When *Gentlemen* occaſionally come toge- ther, why ſhould not their *Converſation* be agree- able to their Superiour Quality ? Methinks they ſhould reckon it beneath People of their Qua- lity to Employ their *Converſation* with one ano- ther on trifling *Impertinencies* ; or at ſuch a rate, that if their Diſcourſe were taken down in ſhort- hand by one behind the Hangings, they would bluſh to have it Repeated unto them. *Nihil ſed Nugæ, et Riſus, et verba proferuntur in ventum.* Sirs, It becomes a *Gentleman*, to Entertain his Company, with the Fineſt *Thoughts*, on the Fineſt *Themes* ! But certainly, there cannot be any Subject ſo worthy of a *Gentleman* as this ; *What Good there is to be done in the World ?* Were this

noble

noble Subject oftner Started in the Conversation of *Gentlemen,* an incredible Deal of *Good* would be done.

I will conclude with Saying, you must *come forth* to any *Publick Service* whereof you may be capable, when you are call'd unto it. Honest *Jeans* has a Pungent Passage ; *The World applauds the Politick Retiredness of those that bury their Parts and Gifts, in an obscure Privacy, tho' both from God and Man, they have a fair call to Publick Employment ; But the terrible censure of these men by Christ at the last Day, will discover them to be the arrantest Fools, that ever were upon the Face of the Earth.* That Fault of not Employing ones Parts for the Publick, One calls, *A Great Sacriledge in the Temple of the God of Nature.* It was a Sad Age, wherein *Tacitus* tells, *Inertia fuit Sapientia.*

§ 20. YOu may Remember, That One of the First of our PROPOSALS was, For EVERY ONE, to consider, *What is there that I may do for the Service of God, and the Welfare of Man ?* 'Tis to be Expected, That all OFFICERS, *As such,* will conform, to what has been thus Proposed. It should be the concern of all *Officers,* from the *Emperour* to the *Enomotarch, To do all the Good they can.* So then, there is the less Need of making a more Particular Application to *Lesser Officers* of several Sorts, who have *Opportunities to Do Good,* more or less, in every one of their hands. However, they shall not All of
them

them, complain that we have Neglected them.

In the CHURCH, fometimes there are 𝕰𝖑𝖉𝖊𝖗𝖘, (as in the Primitive Times, *Ecclefia Seniores habuit,*) who *Rule well, tho' they Labour not in the Word and Doctrine.* It becomes thefe often to confider ; *What fhall I do, to prevent the rife of Strife, or of any Sin, that may be a Root of Bitternefs in the Flock? And, that Chrift, and Holinefs may Reign in it ; and the Paftor have his Miniftry Countenanced, Encouraged, and Profpered?* Their *Vifits* of the Flock, and their Endeavours to *Prepare* People for *Special Ordinances,* may be of unknown Advantage to Religion.

There are 𝕯𝖊𝖆𝖈𝖔𝖓𝖘, Entrufted with the *Temporal Affairs* of the Society. It would be well, if thefe would oftner confider ; *What may I do, that the Treafury of Chrift may be increafed?* And, *What may I do, that the Life of my faithful Paftor may be more comfortable to him!* And, *whom of the Flock do I think defective in their Contributions to Support the Evangelical Interefts, and what fhall I Speak with Great Boldnefs in the Faith unto them?*

In the STATE, there are many *Officers,* to whom the moft Significant and Comprehenfive PROPOSAL, that can be made, would be, *To Confider their* OATHES? If they would Serioufly *Ponder,* and faithfully *Perform,* what their 𝕯𝖆𝖙𝖍𝖊𝖘, oblige 'em to, a Deal of *Good* would be done.

But we muft a little Particularize.

The 𝕽𝖊𝖕𝖗𝖊𝖘𝖊𝖓𝖙𝖆𝖙𝖎𝖛𝖊𝖘 of any Place ; as they

---

they have Opportunities to *Do Good* for the whole People ; and ſhould accordingly think, *What Motions to make?* So they ſhould be Particularly Sollicitous for the *Good* of that Place, which has Elected them.

Thoſe whom we call, The 𝕾𝖊𝖑𝖊𝖈𝖙=𝖒𝖊𝖓 of a Town, will fail a juſt Expectation, if they do not inquiſitively conſider this Point ; *What ſhall I do, that I may be a Bleſſing to the Town, which I am now to Serve?*

𝕲𝖗𝖆𝖓𝖉=𝕵𝖚𝖗𝖞=𝖒𝖊𝖓, may very profitably Conſider ; *What Growing Evils or Nuſance, do I diſcover, whereof I ſhall do well to Procure a Preſentation?* They ſhould hold their *Conſultations,* upon this matter, as Men in Earneſt for the *Good* of the Country.

Indeed, all *Jury-men* ſhould be, *Boni Homines,* that is to Say, *Good Men.* Our Old Compellation of a Neighbour, by the Title, of, *Goodman,* was of this Original ; As much as to ſay, One Qualified to *Serve on a Jury.* But then, let them *Do Good;* and Contrive, How they may do it.

Why ſhould 𝕮𝖔𝖓𝖘𝖙𝖆𝖇𝖑𝖊𝖘 be Excuſed *!* Their Name, [*Conſtabularius*] firſt came, from the care of *Making unruly Horſes to Stand well together in the Stable.* Sirs, Tis very much *Good* that you have to do, by being *Maſters of Reſtraint,* in your Walks, and otherwiſe, unto *unruly Cattle.* What are Vicious People, (tho' Perhaps *in Honour,*) but *like the Beaſts?* Well-diſpoſed *Conſtables* in a Place, have done wondrous Things, to keep up *Good Order.*

Order in it. Your Thoughts on, *What Good may I do?* And, your *Confultations,* I befeech you!

And where 𝕮𝖎𝖙𝖍𝖎𝖓𝖌-𝖒𝖊𝖓 are Chofen and Sworn, 'tis more than a little *Good,* which they may do, if they will confcientioufly do their *Duty.* Let them Study well the *Laws,* which lay down their *Duty* ; and let them alfo often Confider, *What Good may I do?* And confult with one another at certain times, to find out what they have to do, and affift and ftrengthen one another, in the doing of it.

I have done with the *Civil Lift.*

𝕸𝖎𝖑𝖎𝖙𝖆𝖗𝖞 𝕮𝖔𝖒𝖒𝖆𝖓𝖉𝖊𝖗𝖘, have their Opportunities to *Do Good.* They do it very much, when they uphold *Exercifes of Piety,* in their feveral *Regiments* and *Companies.* And when they Rebuke the *Vices of the Camp,* with a due Severity. Might not *Societies to Supprefs thofe Vices,* be formed in the Camp, to very Good Purpofe, under their Infpection ? --- But if the *Souldiers* ask, *What fhall we do?* All my Anfwer at prefent, is only ; *Sirs, Confider what you have to do.*

𝕮𝖔𝖒𝖒𝖆𝖓𝖉𝖊𝖗𝖘 𝖆𝖙 𝕾𝖊𝖆, have their Opportunities too. The more *Abfolute* they are in their Command, the Greater their Opportunities. The *Worfhip of God* Serioufly & Conftantly Maintained aboard, will be of *Good* confequence. A *Body of Good Orders,* hung up in the Steeridge, and carefully Executed, may prove that which all the People of the Veffel may at laft fee caufe to be very thankful for. *Books of Piety*

Piety should alſo be taken aboard, and the men be call'd upon to Retire for the Peruſal thereof, and for other Pious Actions.

But while our Book ſeems to have ſo far diſcharged its Office and Purpoſe of, *A Counſellor,* as to leave no further Expectations, there Preſent themſelves a Conſiderable Number of Perſons, who may juſtly Complain of it, if among PROPOSALS to *Do Good,* they be left Unconſidered. Some whom we do not find among them that Addreſſed the Bleſſed *Morning-Star* of our Saviour, for his Direction, yet are now found among thoſe who Enquire ; *And what ſhall we do?* The Gentlemen of the LAW, who have that in their hands, the End whereof is, *To Do Good;* and the Perverſion of which from its Profeſſed End, is one of the *Worſt of Evils.*

Gentlemen, Your Opportunities to *Do Good,* are ſuch, and ſo Liberal, and Gentlemanly, is your Education, [For even for the Common Pleaders at the Bar, I hope, that Maxim of the Law, will not be forgotten ; *Dignitas Advocatorum non patitur ut in eam recipiatur, qui antea fuerat Vilioris Conditionis :*] that PROPOSALS of what you *may do,* cannot but Promiſe themſelves an Obliging Reception with you. Tis not come to ſo ſad a paſs, That an *Honeſt Lawyer,* may as of old, the *Honeſt Publican,* require a Statue, meerly on the Score of *Rarity.* You may, if you Study it, come to do ſo, on the Score of Univerſal & Meritorious *Uſefulneſs.*

In

In order to your being *Useful,* Sirs, tis neceffary that you be *Skilful.* And that you may arrive to an Excellent *Skill in the Law,* you will be
well advifed, what *Authors* to Study ; *With the
Well-advifed* in this Point, there may be more
than a little *Wifdom.* The Knowledge of your
own *Statute-Law,* is inconteftably needful ; and
fo, of the *Common-Law,* which continually muft
accompany the Execution of it. Here (befides
needful *Dictionaries*) you have your *Cooks,* and
your *Vaughans,* and your *Windgates,* and your
Daltons, and your *Kebles ;* and as many more, as
you have Time to Converfe withal. I am forry
to find a Gentleman about the middle of the former Century Complaining about the *Englifh Law,*
That the *Books of it cannot be Read over, under Three
or Four Years, with any Deliberation ; and that at an
ordinary rate they Coft above Twenty Pounds.* I do
not propound fo long and hard a Task. For the
Civil Law muft alfo be known by them that
would be well acquainted with *Legal Proceedings*
Volumns, huge ones and Cartloads of them, have
been Written upon it ; but among all thefe, methinks at leaft thofe two little ones ; the *Enchiri-
dion* of *Corvinus,* and *Arthur Ducks* Treatife, *De
ufu et Authoritate Juris Civilis;* ought to be Confulted, yea, Digefted, by one that would not be
an *Ignoramus.* I will be yet a little more free,
in declaring my Opinion. Had I Learning
enough to manage a Caufe of that nature, fo
fhould be very ready to maintain it at any *Bar*
in

in the World, That there never was known under the Cope of Heaven, a more Learned man,
than the Incomparable ALSTEDIUS. He has
Written on every one of the Subjects in the whole
Circle of Learning, as Accurately and as Exquisite-
ly as thofe men, who have fpent all their Lives
in Cultivating but any one of the Subjects. The
only Reafon, why his Compofures are no more
Efteemed, is, the *Pleonafm* of his Worth, and their
Deferving fo much Efteem. To hear fome Silly
and Flafhy men, with a Scornful Sneer talk as if
they had fufficiently done his Bufinefs, by a
Foolifh Pun of, *All's Tedious,* is to fee the Un-
grateful and Exalted Folly of the World ; for,
Concifenefs is one of his Peculiar Excellencies ;
They might more juftly call him any thing than
Tedious. This Digreffion only ferves to intro-
duce a Recommendation of this Excellent mans,
Jurifprudentia, as one of the beft Things a *Lawyer*
can be acquainted withal. I fhall wrong it, if
I fay, *Tis Much in a Little* ; I muft fay, *Tis All at
Once.*

A *Lawyer* fhould be a *Scholar.* It Vexes one,
that the Emperor *Juftinian,* whofe Name is now
upon the *Laws* of the Roman Empire, (becaufe
'twas by his Order *Tribonian* made his *Hafty,* and
fome fay *Fallacious* and *Unfaithful* Collection of
them, from the Two Thoufand Volumns, into
which they had been growing for above a Thoufand Years:) is by *Suidas* called, Ανελφαβητ⊕, *One
that fcarce knew his Alphabet.* It is a Vexation to
find

find *Accurfius*, one of the Firſt Gloſſators on the *Laws*, fall into ſo many Groſs miſtakes, thro' his Ignorance ; and unable to afford, when a Sentence of Greek occurs in the Text, any bet-terGloſs than this; *Hæc Graica funt, quæ nec Legi, nec intelligi Poſſunt.* Tho' the thing were a Tri-fle, it was no honour unto thoſe Writers on the *Pandect*, that they knew not what Gender the Name was of. It is odd, that when one Title of the *Law* is, *Of the Signification of words,* the great Interpreter of it, ſhould leave it as a Maxim, *De Verbebus non curat Juris Confultus.* However, a *Bartolus* has not ſo Roughen'd your Study, as a *Budæas* has Poliſh'd it.

But, Sirs, When you are called upon to be *Wiſe*, the main Intention is, *That you may be wiſe to do Good.* Without a Diſpoſition for this, *Doth not their Excellency which is in them go away? They Dy even without Wiſdom.* A Foundation of *Piety* muſt be firſt laid ; An Inviolable Reſpect unto the *Holy and Juſt and Good Laws* of the Infinite GOD. This muſt be the Rule of all your Actions ; and it muſt particularly Regulate your *Practice of the Law.* You are ſenſible, that it was ever the Style of the *Civil Law,* to begin, *A Deo Optimo Maximo.* Nor was it unuſual for the In-ſtruments of the Law, to begin with ΧΡ, the two firſt Letters, abbreviating the Name of ΧΡΙϲΤΟϹ, for which the Notaries have ignorantly Subſti-tuted an [*X.P.*] of later Times. The Life of the *Lawyer* ſhould have its beginning there, and be

carried

carried on with an Eye thither. The Old *Saxon Laws*, had the TEN Great Precepts of the *Decalogue* prefixed in the Front of them : *Ten Words*, in *two Tables* of infinitely more Account than the Famous *Twelve Tables*, that were fo admired by *Tully*, and by other Antiquity ; in the Fragments whereof collected by your *Balduin* and others, there are yet fome things horribly Unrighteous and Barbarous. Thefe are to be the *Firft Laws* with you : and as all the *Laws* that are contrary to thefe, are *ipfo facto* null and void ; So in the *Practice of the Law*, every thing that is Difallow'd by thefe, is to be avoided. The man whom the Scripture calls, *A Lawyer*, was a *Karaite*, or one who kept clofe to the *Written Law* of God, in oppofition to the *Pharifee*, and the *Traditionift*. I know not why every *Lawyer*, fhould not ftill be in the beft fenfe, a *Karaite*. By Expreffing a *Reverence for the Divine Law*, both that of *Reafon*, and that of fuperadded *Gofpel*, you will Do Good in the world, beyond what you can imagine. You will Redeem your honourable Profeffion from the wrong which *Ill Men* have done to the Reputation of it ; And you will obtain another Patronage for it, than what the Satyr in the Idle Story of your Saint *Evona* has affigned it.

Your Celebrated *Ulpian*, wrote Seven Books, to fhow the feveral *Punifhments*, which ought to be inflicted on *Chriftians*. It is to be hoped, that you will invent as many *Services* to be done unto the *Caufe of Chriftianity* ; Services to be done for
L   the

the Kingdom of your Saviour ; and Methods to demonſtrate your own being among the *Beſt of Chriſtians.*

I am not ſure, our *Tertullian* was the Gentleman of that Name, who hath ſome *Conſulta* in the Roman *Digeſta :* Some writers of his Life (as well as *Grotius*) will not have it ſo. Yet *Euſebius* tells us, he was well skilled in the *Roman Laws.* And in his Writings you have many *Law-terms ;* particularly, *Preſcriptions* (the Title of his Treatiſes againſt *Hereticks*) were, as we learn from *Quintilian* and others, the *Replies* of *Defendents,*to the Actions of the *Plaintiffs.* I propoſe, That others of the Faculty, Study all poſſible *Preſcriptions* againſt them, who would hurt Chriſtianity, and *Apologies* for the Church and Cauſe of our Saviour. But, Sirs, It muſt firſt of all be done, in your own Vertuous, Exact, Upright Conduct, under all Temptations.

The Miſcarrriages of ſome Individuals, muſt not bring a Blemiſh, on a Noble and Uſeful Prefeſſion.

But many-will be ready enough,to allow of a Cenſure occurring in a late Book Entituled, *Examen Miſcellaneum :* (and I know ſcarce any thing elſe worth Quoting from it :) *A Lawyer that is a Knave, deſerves Death; more than a Band of Robbers ; for he Profanes the Sanctuary of the Diſtreſſed, and Betrayes the Liberties of the People.* To ward off ſuch a Cenſure, a *Lawyer* muſt ſhun all thoſe *Indirect Ways* of *Making Haſt to be Rich,* in which

which a man cannot be *Innocent* : Such as provoked the Father of Sir *Matthew Hale,* to give
over the *Practice of the Law,* becaufe of the Extreme Difficulty to preferve a *Good Confcience* in
it. Sir, Be prevailed withal, to keep conftantly
a *Court of Chancery* in your own Breaft ; and Scorn
and Fear to do any thing, but what your *Confcience* will pronounce, Confiftent with, yea,
Conducing to, *Glory to God in the Higheft, on Earth
Peace, Good-will towards men.* The very Nature
of your Bufinefs, leads you to Meditations on a
Judgment to come. Oh ! That you would fo Realize and Antedate that *Judgment,* as to do nothing, but what you may verily Believe, will be
approved in it !

This Piety muft Operate very particularly,
in the *Pleading of Caufes.* You will abhor, Sir,
to appear in a *Dirty Caufe.* If you difcern, that
your *Client* has an *Unjuft Caufe,* you will faithfully advife him of it. *Utrum Fallacijs et Decep-
tionibus ad Convincendum Adverfarium uti Liceat ?*
This is the Queftion. Tis to be hoped, That you
have determined it like an *Honeft Man.* You will
be Sincerely defirous, *Truth* and *Right* may take
place. You will fpeak nothing that fhall be to
the Prejudice of *Either.* You will abominate
the ufe of all unfair Arts, to Confound *Evidences,*
to Browbeat *Teftimonies,* to Supprefs what may
give Light in the Cafe. You have nothing a-
gainft that old Rule of Pleading a Caufe; *Cog-
nita Iniquitate, a Sufcepto Ejus Patrocinio Advocatus
defiftere debet.*   L 2   I.

I Remember *Schufterus,* a Famous *Lawyer* and *Counfellor,* who Died at *Heidelberg,* A. C. 1672. had one admirable ftroke in his Epitaph ;

Morti proximus Vocem emifit ;
    Nibil fe unquam fuafiffe confilio,
Cujus jam jam Moriturum peniteret.

A *Lawyer* who can go out of the world with fuch Expreffions, were a greater Bleffing to the World, than can be Expreffed.

I cannot Encourage any Gentleman, to fpend much Time in the Study of the *Canon-Law* : which *Baptifta à Sanéto Blafio,* finds to Contradict the *Civil Law* in Two Hundred Inftances. The *Decrees,* and the *Decretals,* and the *Clementines* and *Extravagants,* which Compofe the hideous Volumns of that *Law,* would compel any Wife man, to make the Apology, that one fuch made, for his Averfion thereunto ; *Non poffum, Domine, vefci ftercore humano. Agrippa,* who was a *Doétor* thereof, faid of that *Law, Tis neither of God, nor for Him ; Nothing but Corruption invented it ; Nothing but Avarice has Praétifed it. Luther* began the *Reformation* with Burning of it. Neverthelefs, there is one Point in the *Canon Law* much infifted on, which well deferves very much of your Confideration ; That is, *Reftitution.* When men *Get Riches and not by Right,* or have heaped up Wealth in any *Difhoneft* and *Criminal* ways, a *Reftitution* will be a Neceffary and Effential Ingredient of that *Repentance,* which alone will find

Ac-

Acceptance with Heaven. The Awe of this Thought may ftand like an *Angel with a Drawn Sword* in your way, when you may be under Temptation to go out of your way after the *Wages of Unrighteoufnefs.* Our *Law* was once given unto us in *French.* Many of you, Gentlemen, ken the *Modern French* as well as the *Ancient.* Monfier *Placette* has given you a Valuable Treatife, of **Reſtitution.** In his Treatife, there is a Chapter, *Des cas ou les Advocats font obliges à Reftituer.* In that Chapter there are fome who will find a fad *Bill of Cofts Taxed* for them. And among other very true Affertions, this is one ; *S'il Exige une Recompenfe Exceffive et difproportionée à ce qu'il fait, il eft obligé à Reftituer ce qu'il prend de trop.* In plain Englifh; *Exceffive Fees* muft be difgorged by **Reſtitution.** It fhould be thought upon.

There has been an old Complaint, *That a Good Lawyer feldom is a Good Neighbour.* You know how to Confute it, *Gentlemen,* by making your *Skill in the Law,* a Bleffing to your Neighourhood. It was affirm'd and foretold as long ago as old *Salluft ; Sine Confidicis fatis fælices olim fuere, futuræque funt urbes.* You may, *Gentlemen,* if you pleafe, be a vaft Acceffion to the *Felicity* of your Countreys.

You fhall have fome of my PROPOSALS for it, in an Hiftorical Exhibition. In the Life of Mr. *John Cotton,* there is related this Paffage concerning his Father, who was a *Lawyer*

L 3   'That

'That worthy man was very Singular, in
'Two moſt Imitable Practices. One was,That
'when any of his Neighbours, deſirous to Sue
'one another, addreſſed him for *Counſel,* it was
'his manner, in the moſt Perſwaſive and Obli-
'ging Terms that could be, to Endeavour a
'*Reconciliation* between both Parties ; Preferring
'the *Conſolations* of a *Peace-maker,* before all the
'*Fees* that he might have got, by blowing up of
'*Differences.* Another was, That Every Night,
'it was his Cuſtom to *Examine himſelf,* with Re-
'flections on the Tranſactions of the Day paſt ;
'wherein if he found, that he had not either
'*Done Good* unto others, or *Got Good* unto his own
'Soul, he would be as much Grieved, as ever
'the Famous *Titus* was, when he could Com-
'plain in the Evening, *Amici, Diem per-*
'*didi.*

What a Noble Thing would it be for you,to
find out Oppreſſed *Widows,*and *Orphans,* and ſuch
as can appear no otherwiſe than, *In forma Pau-*
peris ; Objects in whoſe Oppreſſion, *Might over-*
comes Right ; and Generouſly *Plead their Cauſe?*
Deliver the Poor and Needy, rid them out of the hand
of the Wicked. It will be a Glorious and a God-
like Action!

Wealthy People going to make their *Wills,*
often ask your Advice. You may take the Opportunity to Adviſe them, unto ſuch Liberali-
ties upon *Pious Uſes,* as may greatly advance the
Kingdom of God in the World.

And,

And, when you have an Opportunity by *Law* to Refcue, *The Things that are God's,* from the Sacrilegious Hands of the men that would *Rob God,* it is to be hoped, you will do it with all poffible Generofity and Alacrity.

O Excellent Imitation of our Glorious **ADVOCATE** in the Heavens!

Is there nothing to be mended in the *Laws?* Perhaps, you may difcover many things yet wanting in the *Laws; Mifchiefs* in the Execution and Application of the *Laws,* which ought to be better provided againft ; *Mifchiefs* annoying of Mankind, againft which no *Laws* are yet provided. The *Reformation of the Law,* and more *Law* for the *Reformation of the World,* is what is mightily called for. I don't fay, The *Laws* can be fo *Reduced,* that like thofe of *Geneva,* Five Sheets of Paper may hold them all ; but certainly the *Laws* may be fo *Corrected,* that the World may more Senfibly and Generally feel the Benefit of them. If fome *Lawyers* that are *Men of an Excellent fpirit,* would Employ their Thoughts this way, and bring their Thoughts to pafs in a *Parlaimentary* way, all the World might fare the better for them. An Honeft Gentleman more than Fifty Years ago, wrote an, *Examen Legum Angliæ,* worthy to be taken at this Day, into your Confideration.

Your Learning often Qualifies you to *Write Excellent Things,* not only in your own Profeffion, but alfo on all the Entertaining and Edifying

L 4 Themes

Themes in the World. The Books that have been Written by Learned *Lawyers*, would for Number almoſt Equal an *Alexandrian* Library. Judge by a *Freberus*'s Catalogues, or, by a *Pryns* Performances. What Rare and Rich Books, have been Written by an *Hale*, by a *Grotins*, and by a *Selden* ? Sirs, You may *Plead the Cauſe of Religion*, and of the *Reformation*, by your well-directed Pens ; and you may do Innumerable Services. There is one at this Day, who in his, *Hiſtory of the Apoſtles Creed*, and his Accounts of the *Primitive Church*, has Obliged us to ſay, *That he has offered as a* KING *to the Temple of the King of Heaven*. May the *Lord his God Accept* him !

I muſt now break off.

If you be called, Sir, to the Adminiſtration of Juſtice, in the Quality of a 𝕵𝖚𝖉𝖌𝖊, you will preſcribe to your ſelf *Rules*, like thoſe, which the Renowned Lord Chief Juſtice *Hale*, ſo Religiouſly obſerved, as to become a bright Example for all that Sit in the Seat of Judicature. The Sum of his, were ;

' That Juſtice be adminiſtred, *Uprightly, De-*
' *liberately, Reſolutely.*

' That I reſt not on my own *Underſtanding*, but
' implore the *Direction* of GOD.

' That in the Execution of Juſtice, I carefully
' lay aſide my own *Paſſions*, and not give way to
' them, however provoked.

' That I be wholly Intent on the Buſineſs I
' am about.

' That

' That I suffer not my self to be Prepossessed
' with any Judgment at all, till all the Business,·
' and both Parties are heard.

Of such *Methods*, to *Do Good*, and Serve the
Cause of *Righteousness*, & bring on the Promised
Age, wherein the *People shall be Righteous*,the very
least of all the Glorious Recompences, will be
the Establishment of your Profession, in such a
Reputation, as very many Incomparable Persons
in it have deserved ; and the most Prejudiced
People in the world, Enquiring after the Ble-
mishes of it, must be forced only to bring in an,
Ignoramus.

§ 21. **Reforming-Societies**,or *Societies
for the Suppression of Disorders*, have
begun to grow somewhat into Fashion ; and it
is one of the best *Omens* that the World has upon
it. *Behold,how great a Matter a little* of this Heavenly *Fire* may Kindle! Five or Six Gentlemen
in *London*, began with an Heroic Resolution,&
Association, to Encounter the Torrent of Wick-
edness, which was carrying all before it in the
Nation. More were soon added unto them ;
and tho' they met with great Opposition, from
Wicked Spirits, and these *Incarnate* as well as *Invisible*,and some in *High Places* too, yet they pro-
ceeded with a most honourable and invincible
Courage. Their *Success*, if not proportionable
to their *Courage*, yet was far from *Contemptible.*
In the *Punishments* inflicted on them who trans-
gressed

greffed the Laws of *Good Morality*, there were foon offered many Thoufands of *Sacrifices*, unto the Holinefs of GOD. Hundreds of *Houfes* which were the *Chambers* of Hell, and the *Scandals* of Earth, were foon Extinguifhed. There was a Remarkable Check foon given to raging *Profanity*; and the *Lords-Day* was not openly and horribly Profaned as formerly. And among other *Effays to Do Good*, they Scattered Thoufands of *Good Books*, that had a Tendency to Reform the Evil Manners of the People. It was not long before this Excellent Example was followed in other parts of the *Britifh* Empire. Vertuous men of diverfe Qualities and Perfwafions, became the Members of the *Societies*: Perfons High and Low, Con and Non-con, United; the Union became Formidable to the Kingdom of Darknefs. The Report of the *Societies* flew over the Seas; the Pattern was follow'd in other Country's; Men of Wifdom in Remote Parts of *Europe* have made their joyful Remark upon them, *That they caufe Unfpeakable Good, & annunciate a more illuftrious State of the Church of God, which is to be Expefted, in the Converfion of Jews and Gentiles.* America too, begins to be Irradiated with them!

I will Recite an Account formerly offered unto the Publick, of what may be done by fuch **Societies.**

' What incredible Advantages would arife unto *Re-*
' *ligion*, from **Reforming-Societies**, if the Difpofition to
' them fhould not fall under unhappy Languifhments?
' And if *Religion* flourifh, and *Iniquity* dare no longer
                                                        fhow

' fhow itsHead, what *Profperity* of every Kind,&in every
' Thing, would be the Confequence : A fmall 𝖘𝖔𝖈𝖎𝖊𝖙𝖞
' may prove an Incomparable and Invaluable Bleffing
' to a Town, whofe Welfare fhall become the Object
' of their Watchful Enquiries : They may be as a *Gar-*
' *rifon* to defend it from the worft of its Enemies : They
' may quickly render it, *A Mountain of Holinefs, and a*
' *Dwelling of Righteoufnefs,* that fhall Enjoy the moft
' Gracious Prefence of the Lord. The *Society* may do
' Confiderable things towards the Execution of Whole-
' fome *Laws,* whereby *Vice* is to be difcouraged. *Of-*
' *fendors* againft thofe *Laws* may be kept under fuch
' a Vigilant Infpection, that they fhall not efcape a due
' *Chaftifement* for their Offences. The Effects of fuch
' a Chaftifement may be, that the Rebuked and Cen-
' fured Sinners will be Reclamed from their Sins ; or,
' however, the Judgments of God, which would break
' forth where fuch things are Indulged, will be Di-
' verted. *Ubi Judicium, ibi non eft Judicium. Swearing*
' and *Curfing* will not infect the *Air*; Men will not Reel
' along the Streets,turn'd into *Swine* by their *Cups.*The
' Cages of *UncleanBirds* will be diffipated. They whom
' *Idlenefs* renders Dead while they Live, will have an
' Honeft Employment ordered for them,whereby they
' may Earn an Honeft Livelihood. And the *Lords-*
' *Day* will Vifibly be kept *Holy to the Lord*; which one
' thing will foon Irradiate a Place. with a moft lovely
' *Holinefs* and *Happinefs.* *Vice* is a Cowardly Thing ; it
' will wonderfully fhrink before thofe that will Vifibly
' go to make Head againft it. If any *Laws* to Regu-
' late what is amifs, be yet wanting, the *Society* may
' procure the *Legiflative Power* to be fo addrefs'd, that
' all due Provifion will foon be made by our Law-gi-
' vers. What isDefective in the *By-Laws* of theTown,
' may be by the *Society,* fo obferved, that the Town
' fhall be foon advifed, and the thing redreffed. The
Choice

' Choice of fuch *Officers* as may be Faithful and Ufe-
' ful to the Publick, may be very much influenced by
' the *Society.* If any fort of Men, are notorioufly De-
' fective in their Duty, the *Society* may by directing
' *Admonitions* and *Remonftrances* unto them foon procure
' the Defects to be amended. If any *Families* live
' without *Family-Worfhip,*the *Society* may tell their *Paftor*
' of them, and pray him to Vifit them, and Exhort
' them, and Perfwade them, to continue no longer in
' their *Paganifm* and *Atheifm* ; or, if any are like to
' be Led away by Seducers, or other Temptations, a
' Care may in this way be taken of them. *Schools* of
' all Kinds, may in many Kinds fare the better for the
' *Society* ; [And *Charity-Schools* be Erected, Infpected,
' and Supported.] BOOKS that have in them the
' *Salt* of Heaven, may by means of the *Society* be
' Sprinkled all over the Land ; and the *Savour of Truth*
' be difperfed about the Countrey. Finally ; The *So-*
' *ciety* may find out, who are in Extreme Neceffities,
' and may either by their own Liberality,or by that of
' others to whom they fhall Commend the matter, ob-
' tain Succours for the Neceffitous.

' We know, That a Small *Society* may do fuch
' Things, becaufe to our Knowledge, it has already
' done them ; and yet, it has been concealed from the
' Knowledge of the world, who they were which did
' them. And with Minds that have any *Generofity* or
' *Ingenuity* in them, Elevating them above the *Dregs of*
' *Mankind,* there will need no other Argument for the
' Production of fuch a *Society,*than the Profpect of fuch
' Excellent Things. Thefe are Things that will
' Mightily Commend themfelves unto the Thoughts
' of Well-inclined men ; and they will Eafily fee it
' their *Honour,* to be of a *Society* that will Purfue fuch
' Excellent Ends.

The

The Repetition of thefe Paffages, is enough to make way for the PROPOSAL ;

That a Fit Number in a Neighbourhood, whofe Hearts God has touched with a *Zeal to Do Good,* would Combine into a *Society,* to meet, when & where they fhall agree ; and Confider that Cafe, *What are the* 𝔇𝔦𝔰𝔬𝔯𝔡𝔢𝔯𝔰 *that we may fee Rifing among us ? And what may be done, either by our felves immediately, or by others thro' our Advice, to Suppreß thofe Diforders ?* That they would obtain if they can, the Prefence of a *Minifter* with them ; and every time they meet, have a *Prayer* wherein the Glorious Lord fhall be call'd upon, to Blefs the Defign, Direct and Profper it. That they would alfo have a *Juftice of Peace,* if it may be, to be a Member of the Society. That they once in half a Year Choofe two *Stewards,* to difpatch the *Bufineffes* and *Meffages* of the *Society,* and manage the *Votes* in it ; who fhall Nominate unto the *Society* their Succeffors, when their Term is Expired. That they would have a Faithful *Treafurer,* in whofe Hands their *Stock of Charity* may be depofited : And a *Clerk,* to keep a convenient *Record* of *Tranfactions* and *Purpofes.* And, finally, That they do with as *Modeft* and *Silent* a Conduct as may be, carry on all their Undertakings.

In a Town accommodated with feveral fuch *Societies,* it has been an Ufage, that *Once a Year,* they have met, all of them together, in one Place, and have had a *Day of Prayer,* in which
they

they have *Humbled* themſelves for doing ſo little Good, and beſought the *Pardon* of their *Unfruit-fulneſs*, thro' the Blood of the *Great Sacrifice* ; and implored the *Bleſſing* of Heaven on the *Eſſays to Do Good*, which they have made, and the *Counſel* and *Conduct* of Heaven, for their further Eſſays ; and ſuch Influences of Heaven, as may bring a-bout thoſe *Reformations*, which it was not in their Power to accompliſh.

I will finiſh the PROPOSAL, by Reciting the **Points of Conſideration** which the SO-CIETIES may have Read unto them from time to time at their Meetings, with a due *Pauſe* upon each of them, for any one to offer what he pleaſe upon it.

I. ' **I**S there any **Remarkable Diſorder** in the Place, ' that requires our Endeavour for the Suppreſ-' ſion of it ? And in what Good, Fair, likely way, ' may we Endeavour it ?

II. ' Is there any **Particular Perſon**, whoſe *Diſ-' orderly Behaviours* may be ſo Scandalous & ſo Noto-' rious, that we may do well to ſend unto the ſaid ' Perſon our Charitable *Admonitions* ? Or, Are there ' any *Contending Perſons*, whom we ſhould Admoniſh, ' to Quench their *Contentions* ?

III ' Is there any *Special Service* to the Intereſts of ' Religion. which we may conveniently deſire our ' **Miniſters**, to take notice of ?

IV ' Is there any thing, which we may do well to ' Mention and Recommend unto the **Juſtices**, for the ' further Promoting of *Good Order* ?

V ' Is there any Sort of **Officers** among us, to ſuch ' a Degree unmindful of their Duty, that we may do ' well to Mind them of it ? *VI.*

VI. 'Can any further Methods be devifed, that *Ig-*
'*norance* and *Wickednefs* may be more chafed from our
'People in general ? And that 𝕳𝖔𝖚𝖋𝖊𝖍𝖔𝖑𝖉-𝕻𝖎𝖊𝖙𝖞 in
'Particular, may flourifh among them ?

VII. 'Does there appear any Inftance of 𝕺𝖕𝖕𝖗𝖊𝖋𝖋𝖎𝖔𝖓
'or 𝕱𝖗𝖆𝖚𝖉𝖚𝖑𝖊𝖓𝖈𝖊,in the *Dealings* of any Sort of People,
'that may call for our Effayes, to get it Rectified ?

VIII. 'Is there any matter to be humbly moved un-
'to the 𝕷𝖊𝖌𝖎𝖋𝖑𝖆𝖙𝖎𝖛𝖊 𝕻𝖔𝖜𝖊𝖗 to be Enacted into a 𝕷𝖆𝖜
'for Publick Benefit ?

IX. 'Do we know of any Perfon languifhing under
'Sad and Sore 𝕬𝖋𝖋𝖑𝖎𝖈𝖙𝖎𝖔𝖓; And is there any thing that
'we may do, for the Succour of fuch an Afflicted
'Neighbour ?

X. 'Has any Perfon any 𝕻𝖗𝖔𝖕𝖔𝖋𝖆𝖑 to make, for our
'own further Advantage and Affiftence, that we our
'felves may be in a Probable and Regular Capacity,
'to Purfue the 𝕴𝖓𝖙𝖊𝖓𝖙𝖎𝖔𝖓𝖘 before us ?

My Reader, *Look now towards Heaven, and tell
the Stars, if thou be able to Number them,* which the
Telefcopes have already difcovered, and are ftill
to fetch into their Difcovery, befides the *Nine-
teen Hundred,* which are brought down into the
Later Globes ; Yea, Tell firft the Leaves of an
Hercynian Forreft, and the *Drops* of an *Atlantick*
Ocean ; *Then* tell how many *Good Things* may
be done, by 𝕾𝖔𝖈𝖎𝖊𝖙𝖎𝖊𝖘 of Good Men, having
fuch *Points of Confideration* always before them !

And yet, when fuch 𝕾𝖔𝖈𝖎𝖊𝖙𝖎𝖊𝖘 have done
all the Good they can and nothing but **Good,**
and walk on in a more unfpotted *Brightnefs* than
that of the *Moon in Heaven,* let them look to be
Maligned, and Libell'd ; As, *A fet of Scoundrels,*
who

who are Maintain'd by Lying, Serve God for Un-righteous Gain, and Ferret Whores for Subsistence ; and are not more Unanimous against Immorality in their Informations, than for it in their Practice : A-*void no Sins in themselves, and will suffer none in any Body else.* I suppose, they that Publish their Censures on the *Manners of the Age* will express this Malignity, because they *have* done so. Sirs, *Add to your Faith, Courage,* and be Arm'd for such Trials of it!

§ 22. WE will not Propose, That our *Essays to Do Good,* should ever come to an End. But we will now put an End unto this, of Tendring PROPOSALS for it. It shall Conclude with a *Catalogus Desideratorum,* or a mention of some Obvious, and General *Services* for the Kingdom of God among Mankind, whereto 'twere to be desired, that Religious and Ingenious men might be Awakened.

𝕬 𝕮𝖆𝖙𝖆𝖑𝖔𝖌𝖚𝖊 𝖔𝖋 𝕯𝖊𝖘𝖎𝖗𝖆𝖇𝖑𝖊𝖘, waiting for the *Zeal of Good Men* to Prosecute them.

[*Difficilem rem optas ; Generis Humani Innocentiam !*]

I. The Propagation of the Holy and Glorious *Religion of* CHRIST ; a Religion which *Emancipates* Mankind from the worst of Slaveries and Miseries, and wonderfully *Ennobles* it ; and which alone prepares men for the Blessedness of another World: Why is this no more Endeavoured
by

by the Profeſſors of it? PROTESTANTS, why will you be out-done by *Popiſh Idolaters*! Oh! the vaſt Pains which thoſe *Bigots*,have taken, to carry on the *Romiſh* Merchandiſes and Idola-tries! No leſs than Six hundred Clergy-men, in that one order of the *Jeſuites,*did within a Few years, at ſeveral times, Embark themſelves for *China,* to win over that mighty Nation unto their Baſtard-Chriſtianiy. No leſs than Five Hundred of them Loſt their *Lives,* in the Diffi-culties of their Enterprize ; and yet the Survi-vers go on with it; Expreſſing a ſort of Trou-ble,that it fell not unto their Share to make a Sa-crifice of their *Lives,* in Enterpriſing the Propa-gation of Religion. *O my God, I am Aſhamed, & bluſh to Lift up my Face unto thee my God*! It were but a *Chriſtian,* but a *Grateful,* but an *Equal* Thing ; but who can foretel what *Proſperity* might be the Recompence! If our *Companies* and *Factories,* would ſet a part a more conſidera-ble part of their *Gains* for this work, and ſet up-on a more vigorous Proſecution of it. *Gordons* propoſal, unto all men of Eſtates,to Set a part a Small part of their Eſtates for this purpoſe, [At the End of his *Geography,*] ſhould be taken into further conſideration. What has been done by the *Dutch* Miſſionaries at *Ceylon,* and what is do-ing by the *Daniſh* Miſſionaries at *Malabar ;* One would think,might Animate us, to Imitate them !

If Men of a Spirit for *Evangelizing,* and *Illumi-nating* a woful World,would Learn the *Languages*

M   of

of Some Nations that are yet *Ungofpellized,* and wait on the Providence of Heaven, to lead them to, and own them in, Some *Apoftolical Undertakings,* who can tell what might be done? We know, what *Ruffinus* relates concerning the Converfion of the *Iberians ;* and what *Socrates,* concerning the Things done by *Frumentius* and *Ædefius,* in the *Inner India.*

But on this *Defireable* there are Two Things *Remarkable.*

Firft, It is the conjecture of fome *Seers,* That until the *Temple* be *cleanfed,* there will be no General Appearance of the *Nations* to worfhip in it. And the Truth is, There will be Danger, until then, that many Perfons Active in *Societies for the Propagation of Religion,* may be more intent upon Propagating their own Little *Forms* and *Fancies* and *Interefts,* than the more *Weighty matters of the Gofpel.* Yea, t'wil be well, if they be not unawares impofed upon, to hurt *Chriftianity* where 'tis well-Eftablifhed, while places wholly *Ungofpellized* in the Neighbourhood may ly neglected. Let us therefore do what we can towards the Churches *Reformation,* in order to its *Dilatation.*

Secondly, It is probable, That the *Holy Spirit* in Operations, like thofe of the Firft Ages, whereby Chriftianity was firft *Planted,* will be again conferred from our *Afcended Lord,* for the *Spreading* of it. The *Holy Spirit,* who has withdrawn from the *Apoftate Church,* will come, and *Abide* with

with us, and render this World like a *Watered Garden.* His Irrefiſtible Influences, will cauſe whole *Nations* to be *born at once;* He will not only *Convert* but *Unite,* His People. By Him, God ſhall *Dwell with men.* Would not the *Heavenly Father give His Holy Spirit,* if it were more *Asked* of Him!

II. 'Tis Lamentable to See the *Ignorance* and *Wickedneſs,* yet remaining, even in many parts of the *Britiſh* Dominions : In *Wales ;* in the *High-Lands ;* and in *Ireland.* Are the *Gouges* all Dead ? There are pretended *Shepherds,* in the World, that will never be able to Anſwer before the Son of God, for their Laying ſo little to Heart, the *Deplorable* Circumſtances, of ſo many People, whom they might, if they were not Scandalouſly Negligent, bring to be more Acquainted with the only Saviour. And there might be more done, that ſome of the *American* Colonies, may no longer be ſuch *Cimmerian* ones ?

III. Why is no more done, for the Poor *Greeks,* and *Armenians,* and *Muſcovites,* and other Chriſtians, who have little *Preaching,* and no *Printing* among them ? If we ſent *Bibles,* and *Pſalters,* and other *Books of Piety* among them, in their own Languages, they would be *Noble* Preſents, and, God knowes, how *Uſeful* ones !

IV. Poor *Sailours,* and Poor *Souldiers,* call for our Pity. They meet with *Great and Sore Troubles.* Their *Manners* are too commonly ſuch, as diſcover no very Good Effects of their *Troubles.*

M 2   What

What fhall be done to make them a *better fort of men?*
There muft, befides more *Books of Piety* diftributed
among them, other methods be tho't upon; *Cadit*
Afinus et eft qui fublevat. *Perit Anima, et non eft qui*
manum apponat! Let *Auftin* awaken us.

V. The *Trades-mans Library* needs to be more
Enriched. We have feen, *Husbandry Spiritualiz-*
ed; and, *Shepherdy Spiritualized;* and, *Navigation*
Spiritualized; We have feen, the *Weaver* alfo accommodated, with agreeable Meditations. To
Spread the *Nets of Salvation* for men, in the ways
of their *Perfonal Callings,* and convey Good
Thoughts unto them, in the *Terms* and *Steps,* of
their Daily Bufinefs, is a Real Service to the Interefts of Piety. A BOOK alfo, that fhall be an
Onomatologia Monitoria, and fhall advife People
how to make their *Names* become unto them,
the *Monitors* of their Duty; might be of much
ufe to the *Chriftened* World. And, a BOOK,
that fhall be, *The Angel of Bethefda,* and fhall inftruct People how to improve in agreeable Points
of Piety, from the feveral Maladies, which their
Bodies may be Difeafed withal; and at the fame
time, inform them of the moft Experimented,
Natural, Specifick *Remedies* for their Difeafes,
might be very ufeful to Mankind. Thefe Two
Subjects, if not undertaken by any other Hand,
may be fo fhortly by that which now Writes;
Except the Glorious Lord of my Life, immediately put an End unto it; and *my Dayes are paft,*
my Purpofes are broken off, even the Thoughts of my
Heart! VI.

VI. Univerſities that ſhall have more *Collegia Pietatis* in them, like thoſe of the Excellent *Franckius* in the lower *Saxony* ; Oh *!* that there were more of them *! Seminaries* in which the Scholars may have a moſt Polite Education; but not be ſent forth with Recommendations for the Evangelical Miniſtry, till it be upon a ſtrict Examination found, that their Souls are fired with the *Fear* of God, and the *Love* of Chriſt, and a *Zeal* to Do Good, and a *Reſolution* to bear Poverty, and Obloquy, and all ſorts of Temptations, in the Service of our Holy Religion *;* they would be the *Wonders* of the World ; And what *wonders* might they do in the World!

Let the *Charity-Schools* alſo, *Increaſe and Multiply; Charity-Schools,* which may provide Subjects for the Great Saviour, Bleſſings for the next Generation ; *Charity-Schools,* not perverted unto the ill purpoſes of introducing a *Defective Chriſtianity.*

VII. Thoſe things, that ſo far as we *underſtand by the Books* of the Sacred Prophecies, are to be, *The Works of our Day;* Tis *Wiſdom* to Obſerve and Purſue. When the Time was arrived, that the *Antichriſt* muſt Enter his Laſt *Half-Time,* One Poor Monk proves a main Inſtrument of Raviſhing *Half* his Empire from him. Thus to fall in with the Deſigns of the *Divine Providence,* is the way to be wonderfully Proſpered and Honoured. One Small Man, thus *Nicking the Time* for it, may do wonders *!*

I take the *Works of our Day* to be ;

1. The *Reviving of Primitive Chriſtianity*; To Study and Reſtore every thing, of the *Primitive* Character. The *Apoſtaſy* is going off. The Time for *cleanſing the Temple* comes on. More *Edwards*'s would be vaſt Bleſſings, where the *Primitive Doctrines of Chriſtianity* are Depraved.

2. The Perſwading of the *European* Powers, to ſhake off the Chains of *Popery.* This Argument ; There is no *Popiſh Nation*, but what by Embracing the *Proteſtant Religion*, would *ipſo facto*, not only aſſert themſelves into a Glorious *Liberty*, but alſo *Double their Wealth* immediately ; 'Tis Marvellous, that it is no more yet hearkened unto *!* Sirs, Proſecute it, with more of *Demonſtration.* One ſhowes, That the Aboliſhing of Popery in *England*, is worth at Leaſt Eight Millions of Pounds yearly to the Nation. Let the Argument be tried with other Nations ; the Argument, *Ab Utili.*

3 The *Forming* and *Quickning* of that PEO-PLE, that are to be, 𝕿𝖍𝖊 𝕾𝖙𝖔𝖓𝖊 𝕮𝖚𝖙 𝖔𝖚𝖙 𝖔𝖋 𝖙𝖍𝖊 𝕸𝖔𝖚𝖓𝖙𝖆𝖎𝖓. Here, as well as in ſome other Things, *None of the Wicked ſhall underſtand, but the Wiſe ſhall underſtand.* God will do His own Work, in His own Time, and in His own Way. And *Auſtin* tells me, *Utile eſt ut taceatur aliquod verbum*, *Propter Incapaces.*

The

The Conclusion.

THE *Zeal of the Lord of Hosts will Perform these things* : A *Zeal* infpired and produced by the *Lord of Hosts* in His Faithful Servants, will put them upon the Performance of fuch Things. Nothing has been yet Propofed, that is Impra-&ible ; *Non Fortia Loquor, fed Poffibilia.* But, *Eu-febius* has taught me, *Vere magnum eft magna facere, et Teipfum putare nibil.* Sirs, Under and After a Courfe of fuch *Actions,* which have a true Glory in them, and really are more Glorious than all the *Actions* and *Atchievements,* whereof thofe Bloody Plunderers, whom we call, *Conquerors,* have made a wretched Oftentation : and per-haps made Infcriptions like thofe of *Pompey* on his Temple of *Minerva* ; --- Still *Humility,* muft be the *Crown* of all. All, nothing without *Hu-mility* ; nothing without a fenfe that you are *Nothing,* a Confent to be made *Nothing.* You muft firft, moft Humbly Acknowledge unto the Great GOD, *That after you have done all, you are Unprofitable Servants* ; and make your Humble Confeffion, That not only you have *done but that which was your Duty to do,* but alfo that you have exceedingly fallen fhort of doing your *Duty.* If God abafe you with very *Dark Difpenfations* of His Pro-vidence, after all your Indefatigable and your Difintereffed Effays to *Glorify* Him, Humble your felves before Him ; yet abate nothing of your

Effays

Essays ; Hold on, saying, *My God will Humble me,
yet will I Glorify Him. Lord, Thou art Righteous ;
But still I will do all I can to serve thy Glorious Kingdom.* This indeed, is a more easy *Humiliation ;*
but then there is one to be demanded, of much
greater Difficulty ; That is, That you humbly
Submit unto all the *Diminutions,* among *Men,*
that God shall order for you. Your Admirable
Saviour was one who *went about* ever *Doing of
Good ;* Mankind was never Visited by such a *Benefactor.* And yet we read, *He was One spoken a-
gainst.* Never any one so Vilified! Had He been
the worst *Malefactor* in the World, He could not
have been worse dealt withal. He Expostulated,
*For which of my Good Works is it that you treat me
so ?* Yet they went on; They Hated Him, they
Reproached Him, they Murdered Him. *Austin*
said very truly, *Remedium Elationis est contuitus
Dominicæ Crucis.* It will also be the Remedy of
Discouragement ; it will keep you from *Sinking,*
as well as being *Lifted up.* You are Conformed
unto your Saviour, in your Watchful Endeavours to *Do Good,* and be *Fruitful in every Good
Work.* But your Conformity unto Him, yet *Lacks
One thing ;* That is, After all, to be *Despised and
Rejected of Men ;* and Patiently to bear the Contempt, and Malice, and Abuses of an *Untoward
Generation.* One of the Fathers, who sometimes
wanted a little of this Grace, could say, *Nihil est
quod nos ita et Hominibus et Deo Gratos facit. quam
& Vitæ Merito magni, et Humilitate infimi simus.* Tis
an

an Excellent thing to come to *Nothing.* If you
hear the Hopes of Difaffected men, to fee you
come to Nothing, Hear it with as much of Satisfaction as they can *Hope* it. Embrace *Exinani-
tions;* Embrace *Annihilations.* I find a Zealous
and Famous *Doer of Good,* much Affected with
the Picture of a Devout man, to whom a Voice
comes down from Heaven, *Quid vis fieri pro te?*
Whereto he replies, *Nihil, Domine, nifi pati et Con-
temni pro te.* Sirs, Let it be feen fome where elfe
than in *Picture;* be you the *Subftance* of it. Thus,
Let Patience have its Perfect Work!
 I hope, you have more Difcretion, than to
imagine, That becaufe you are never *Weary of
Well-Doing,* therefore you fhould be Univerfally
Well-fpoken of. No; 'Twill be juft the Contrary.
To *Do Well,* and to *Hear Ill,* is the Common Experience, and ought to be our Conftant Expectation. For this moft *Unreafonable* thing, there
are very many *Reafons.* 'Twill be impoffible to
Do much Good, but fome or other will count themfelves *Hurt* by what you do. You will Unavoidably ferve fome *Interefts,* which others are Indif-
pos'd unto. 'Tis alfo in the Nature of *Mad men,*
to take up ftrange Prejudices againft their *Beft
Friends;* to be fet againft None fo much as *Them.*
Now, we may every where fee thofe, concerning whom we are told, *Madnefs is in their Hearts.*
It will appear in their being unaccountably Prejudiced, againft thofe that moft of all feek to *Do
Good* unto them. Then, *He teareth me in his Wrath*
who

*who hateth me ; he gnasheth upon me with his Teeth ;
mine Enemy sharpeneth his Eyes upon me!* Then, to
Skorakizing a *Benefactor*, for nothing in the world,
but becaufe he would have been fo ! He fhall
be Honoured, as the *Lindians* Worfhipped *Her-
cules,* by *Curfing,* and Throwing of *Stones.* The
Wrath of God, againft a Sinful and Woful World,
has likewife its Operation in this Grievous matter. If men always upon *Intentions* and *Inventions* to *Do Good,* were fo Generally Belov'd and
Efteem'd as they might be, they would be *Inftruments* of doing more *Good,* than the Juftice of
Heaven, can yet allow to be done for *Such* a
World. *The World is not worthy* of them, nor of
the *Good* that is Endeavoured by them. To de-
prive the World of that *Good,* they muft be left
unto a ftrange *Averfion* for thofe Men that would
fain do it. This Creeples them, Fetters them,
Defeats their Excellent Purpofes ! Nor is the
Devil Idle on this Occafion. A man who fhall
Do much Good, will therein do much *Harm* unto
the Empire of the *Devil.* It would be much, if
the *Devil* fhould not *feek to Devour,* or take an
Exquifite Revenge upon fuch *Men of God.* Except God lay an Uncommon Reftraint upon
that *Wicked One,* fuch is the *Power of the Adver-
fary,* &fuch an *Energy* the *Devil* has upon the minds
of Multitudes, that he will notably & bitterly *Revenge* himfelf upon any Notable *Doer of Good ;* and
procure him a *Troop* of Enemies, Three Volleys
of Obloquies. But, O Servant of God, *By Him thou
wilt*

wilt run thro' a Troop ; By thy God thou wilt Leap over a Wall. We may be so far from wondring, that *Wicked men* are Violently Disaffected unto a man who does abundance of *Good,* and Spread as many Stories, and Write as many Libels, to his Disadvantage, as ever the incomparable *Calvin* suffered from them ; we may rather wonder that the *Devil* does not make this world hotter than a *Babylonish Furnace* for him ; too hot for his Abiding in it. Sirs, If you will *Do much,* tis very likely that the *Devil* may sometimes raise upon your Opportunities to *Do Good,* such an *Horrible Tempest,* as may threaten a total Ruine unto them. You may fear that you see your *Serviceableness,* the *Apple of your Eye struck out ;* you may be driven to Prayers, to Tears, to *Fasting often* in Secret Places ; Prostrate in the Dust, you must *offer up your Supplications, with strong Crying and Tears,* to Him that is *able to Save* your Opportunities from *Death ;* you must Cry out, *O Deliver my Soul, (my Serviceableness) from the Sword, my Darling, (my Serviceableness) from the Power of the Dog !*

The words of the Great *Baxter,* are Proper & Worthy to be Introduced on this Occasion.

'The *Temptations* and *Suggestions* of *Satan,* yea, and
'oft his External Contrived Snares are such, as fre-
'quently give men a Palpable Discovery of his Agency.
'Whence is it, that such wonderful Successive Trains
'of Impediments, are set in the way of almost any man,
'that intends any Great & Good Work in the World ?
'I have among men of my own Acquaintance observed
'such

' such admirable Fruftrations of many Defigned Ex-
' cellent Works, by fuch ftrange unexpected means, &
' fuch variety of them, and fo powerfully carried on,
' as hath of it felf Convinced me, that there is a moft
' Vehement Invifible Malice permitted by God to Re-
' fift Mankind, and to Militate againft all Good in
' the World. Let a man have any work of Greateft
' Natural Importance, which tends to no Great Benefit
' to Mankind, and he may go on with it, without any
' Extraordinary Impedition. But let him have any
' great Defign for *Common Good*, in things that tend to
' deftroy Sin, to heal Divifions, to Revive Charity, to
' Increafe Vertue, to Save mens Souls ; yea, or to the
' Publick Common Felicity ; and his Impediments
' fhall be fo multifarious, fo far-fetch'd, fo fubtle, fo
' inceffant, and in Defpite of all his Care and Refolu-
' tion, ufually fo Succefsful, that he fhall feem to him-
' felf, to be like a man that is held faft Hand & Foot,
' while he fees no one touch him ; or that fees an hun-
' dred Blocks brought and caft before him in his way,
' while he fees no one to do it.

I tranfcribe this paffage for this purpofe. O
Doer of Good, Expect a Conflict with *Wicked
Spirits in High Places*, to Clog all the Good thou
doft propofe to do ; And Expect that Reftlefs
Endeavours of Theirs, to overwhelm thee with
Vile *Ideas* in the Minds, and *Calumnies* in the
Mouthes, of many People concerning thee, will
be fome of their *Devices* to Defeat all thy *Pro-
pofals*. *Be not Ignorant of the Satanick Devices* !

Yea, and if the *Devil* were Afleep, there is
Malignity Enough, in the Hearts of *Wicked Men*
themfelves, to render a man that will *Do Good*,
very

very Diftaftful and Uneafy to them. They are
the Off-fpring of him, who *Slew his Brother, becaufe his Works were Righteous* ; and they will
Malign a man, becaufe he is Ufeful to other men.
Indeed, *Malis difplicere eft Laudari* : But Wicked
men, will *Curfe* a man, becaufe he is a *Blefling.*
Oh! Bafe and Black Difpofition!

I happened once to be prefent in the Room,
where a Dying man could not Dy till he had
bewayled unto a Minifter whom he had now
therefore fent for, the unjuft *Calumnies* & *Injuries* which he had often caft upon him: The Minifter asked the poor Penitent, what was the occafion of his *Abufivenef* ; whether he had been
by any Mif-reports impos'd upon? The man
made this horrible Anfwer ; *No, Sir* ; *'Twas nothing
but this ; I thought You were a Good Man, and that
You did much Good in the World, and therefore I Hated
You*! Oh! *Is it Poffible, Is it Poffible,* (faid the poor
Sinner,) *for fuch a Sinner to find a Pardon*! Truly,
tho' other Caufes may be pretended for the *Spite*
and *Rage* of Wicked men, againft a *Fruitful Doer
of Good* ; Yet I fhall not be *Deceived*, if I fear, that
oftentimes a fecret *Antipathy* to the *Kingdom of
God*, lies at the Bottom of it. Or it may be fometimes a *Pale Envy*, in Proud men, raging that
other men are more *Ufeful* in the world than they,
and vexing themfelves with worfe than *Sicilian
Torments*, at the fight of what God and man do
for other men. *They fee it and are Grieved.* Sirs,
Non Bonus eft qui non ad Invidiam ufque Bonus eft.
But

But now, for fuch Caufes, you muft not *think
ftrange of the Trial,* if men *Speak Evil of you,* after
you have *Done Good* unto many, yea, unto thofe
very People who *Speak* it. It will not be *ftrange,*
if you fhould *hear the Defaming of Many ;* If the
men who do not Love the *Holy Wayes* of the Lord
in His Churches, have no Love to you ; If never fo many *Ariftephanes's* fall upon you ; If *Ja-
velins* are thrown at you, with a Rage reaching
to Heaven ; And if *Pamphlets* are ftuff'd with vile
Figments and Slanders upon you. God may
wifely permit thefe things, and in much Faith-
fulnefs, *To hide Pride from you.* [*O Quantum eft
venenum fuperbiæ, quod non poteft nifi veneno Curari!*]
Alas, while we carry the *Grave-Cloathes* of *Pride*
ftill about us, thefe rough Hands are the beft that
can be to pull them off *!* If you fhould meet
with fuch Things, you muft bear them with
much *Meekneß,* much *Silence,* Great *Self-Abhorrence,*
and a fpirit to *Forgive,* the worft of all your Per-
fecutors. *Being Defamed,* you muft *Entreat.* Be
Glad, if you can Redeem any Opportunities to
Do Good. Be ready to *Do Good,* even unto thofe
from whom you *Suffer Evil.* And when you
have done all the *Good* that you can, reckon your
felf well Paid, if you efcape as well as the *Crane* did
from the *Wolf,* & if you are not *Punifhed* for what
you do. In fhort, Be infenfible of any *Merits* in
your Performances. Ly in the *Duft,* and be willing that both *GOD* and *Man* fhould lay you
there. Have your Spirit Reconciled unto *Indignities.*
En-

Entertain them with all the *Calmneß,* all the
Temper, imaginable. Be content, That *Three
Hundred* in *Sparta,* fhould be Preferr'd before you.
When Envious People can fix no other Blemifh
on you, they will fay of you, as they faid of
Cyprian, That *You are a Proud Man* ; becaufe you
do not Jog on in their heavy Road of *Slothfulneß.*
Bear this alfo, with yet a more Profound *Hu-
mility.* Tis the Laft Effort ufually made by the
Dying *Pride of Life,* to bear the Charge of *Pride*
impatiently, with a *Proud* impatience.

Ye *Ufeful Men,* Your *Acceptance* with your Saviour, and with God thro' your Saviour, and
Recompence in the World to come, is to carry you
Cheerfully thro' all your *Eſſays* at *Ufefulneß.* To
be *Reprobate for every Good Work,* is a Chara&er,
from which 'twill be the *Wiſdom* of all men, to
fly with all the Dread imaginable. But then, to
be *Always abounding in the work for the Lord,* this is
always the Trueft and the Higheft *Wiſdom.* Tis
the *Wiſdom which is from Above,* that is Full of
Mercy and Good Fruits. The *Sluggards* who Do
no Good in the world, are *Wife in their own Con-
ceit* ; but the Men who are Diligent in *Doing* of
Good, can give fuch a *Reafon* for what they do,
as proves them to be *Really Wife.* Men *Leave
off to be Wife,* when they *Leave off to Do Good.*
The *Wiſdom* of it appears in this ; Tis the beft
way of fpending our *Time* ; tis *Well-ſpent,* when
fpent in *Doing of Good.* It is alfo a fure way, a
fweet way, Effe&ually to Befpeak the *Bleſſings* of
God

God on our felves. Who fo likely to *Find Blef-ings*, as the men that *Are Bleffings*? It has been faid *Qui bene Vivit, femper Orat* ; So I will fay, *Qui bene Agit, bene Orat*. Every *Action* we do for the *Kingdom* of God, is in the Efficacy of it, a *Prayer* for the *Kindneß* of God. While we are *at work* for God, certainly, He will be *at work* for us, & ours : He will do for us, more than ever we have *done* for Him ; Far *more than we can Ask or Think* ! There is a *Voice* in every *Good Thing* that is done ; Tis that, *Oh! Do Good unto them that are Good !* Thus my BONIFACIUS anon comes to wear the Name of BENEDICTUS alfo. Yea, and there may be this more particular Effect of what we do. While we *Employ* our *Wits* for the Interefts of God, it is very probable, that we fhall *fharpen* them for our own. We fhall become the more *Wife for our felves*, becaufe we have been *Wife to do Good*. And of the man who is a *Tree that brings forth Fruit*, we read, *whatfoever he doth fhall Profper*. Nor can a man take a Readier way to *Live Joyfully, all the Days of the Life of our Vanity, which God has given us under the Sun*. For, now our *Life* will not be thrown away in *Vanity*; we don't *Live in Vain*. My Friend, *Go thy way* and be Joyful ; *For God accepteth thy works*. Our *Few & Evil* Dayes, are made much lefs fo, by our *Doing* of *Good* in every one of them, as it rolleth over us. Yea, the Holy *Spirit* of God who is the *Quick-ner* of them who *Do Good without Ceafing*, will be their *Comforter*. Every Day of our *Activity*

for

for the Kingdom of God, will be in some sort a Day of *Pentecost* unto us, a Day of the Holy Spirit's coming upon us. The*Consolations of God,* will *not be small,* with the man, who is full of *Contrivances for God,*& for HisKingdom. In short, We read, *The Valleys are Covered over with Corn ; they shout for Joy, they also Sing.* We may be in *Low* Circumstances : But if we abound in the Fruits of *well-doing,*& if we feed many with ourServices, we are *Covered over with Corn.* We shall *Shout for Joy, & also Sing,* if we be so. The *Conscience* of what we do, & of what we Aim to do, will be a *Continual Feast* unto us. *Our Rejoycing is this, The Testimony of our Conscience !* And, *Recte fecisse Merces est.* Yea, the *Pleasure* in doing of *Good Offices,* tis Inexpressible ; tis Unparallel'd ; tis *Angelical ;* more to be Envied than any *Sensual Pleasure ;* a most *Refined* One. Pleasure was long since defined,*The Result of some Excellent Action.*Tis,a sort of *Holy Epicurism.*O most*Pityable* they that will continue Strangers to it *!* But, *Memineris,*was the constant word of Encouragement unto a Souldier. I say, *Remember ;* there's more to be *Remembred.*

When the *Serviceable* Man comes to his *Nunc Demittis,* then, he who did *Live Desired,* shall *Dy Lamented.* It shall be Witnessed and Remembred of him,*That he was one who did Good in Israel.* An *Epitaph* the Glory whereof is beyond that of the most Superb and Stately *Pyramid !* When the calumniators, who once *Lick'd the File* of his Reputation, shall have only the Impotence of

N   their

their Defeated Malice to reflect upon. And a *Therfites* will not have a more Difadvantageous Article in all his character than this, *That he was an Enemy to fuch an* Ulyffes. But what fhall be done for this Good man in the *Heavenly World?* His *Part* and his *Work* in the *City of God,* is as yet Incomprehenfible unto us. But the *Kindnefs* that his God will fhow unto him, in the *Strong City,* will be *Marvellous! Marvellous!* To make the Exclamation of *Auftin,* Writing, *Of the City; Quanta erit illa fælicitas, ubi nullum erit malum, nullum latebit bonum!* His Effayes to fill this World with *Righteous Things,* are fo many *Tokens for Good* upon him, that he fhall have a *Share* and a *Work,* in that World, wherein fhall *Dwell* nothing but *Righteoufnefs.* He fhall be introduced into that World, with a word from the Mouth of the Glorious JESUS, which will be worth a Thoufand Worlds; *Well done, Good and Faithful Servant!*--- And, Oh! What fhall be done for him! He has done what he could for the *Honour of the King of Heaven;* All fhall be done for him, that may be done for One whom the *King of Heaven delights to honour.*

I will give you All Summed up in one Word; It is that, Prov. 14. 22. 𝕸𝖊𝖗𝖈𝖞 𝖆𝖓𝖉 𝕿𝖗𝖚𝖙𝖍 𝖘𝖍𝖆𝖑𝖑 𝖇𝖊 𝖙𝖔 𝖙𝖍𝖊𝖒 𝖜𝖍𝖔 𝕯𝖊𝖛𝖎𝖘𝖊 𝕲𝖔𝖔𝖉. Children of God, There is a Strain of *Mercy and Truth,* in all the *Good* that you *Devife.* You *Devife* how to deal *Mercifully* and *Truly,* with every one; and bring every one to do fo too.

And

And the *Mercy* & *Truth* of God, now for ever Engaged for you, fhall here Suffer you to *Lack no
Good Thing,* but fhall hereafter do you *Good* beyond what the *Heart of Man,* can yet *conceive.* A
Faithful God, a Saviour who is one *of Great Faith-
fulnefs,* is He that has *Promifed* it *! The Mouth of
the Lord hath fpoken it.*

I have not forgotten the words ufed by the
Excellent *Calvin,* when the order for his Banifh-
ment from Ungrateful *Geneva* was brought unto him. *Certe fi Hominibus Serviviffem, mala mihi
merces perfolveretur ; fed bene eft, quod ei infervivi,
qui nunquam non fervis fuis rependit, quod femel
promifit.* And I will conclude with a TESTI-
MONY that I fhall abide by. Tis this ; Were
a Man able to Write in *Seven Languages :* could
he converfe daily with the Sweets of all the *Liberal Sciences,* that more Polite men ordinarily
pretend unto ; did he entertain himfelf with all
Ancient & Modern *Hiftories;* And could he Feaft
continually on the *Curiofities* which all forts of
Learning may bring unto him ; None of all this
would afford the Ravifhing Satisfaction, much lefs
would any groffer Delights of the *Senfes* do it ;
which he might find, in relieving the Diftreffes of
a Poor, Mean, *Miferable Neighbour ;* and which he
might much more find, in doing any *Extenfive
Service* for the Kingdom of our Great SAVIOUR
in the World ; or any thing to redrefs the Mi-
feries under which Mankind is generally
Languifhing.

AN

An Appendix;
Concerning the ESSAYS that are made, for the **Propagation of Religion** among the Indians, in the *Maſſachuſet*-Province of NEW-ENGLAND.

IT has been deſired, That our Book of **Eſſays to do Good**, may give an Account, of Some that are actually Purſued, on One of the moſt important Articles that have been propoſed. The occaſion for this Deſire, has been given by ſome odd Inſinuations made by ſome who expreſs a Zeal for, *The Propagation of Religion*, as if nothing had been done that way, by any People of our Profeſſion, who readily own, ' That we are for Embracing & Diffuſing the Holy Re-' ligion of CHRIST, in the *Original Purity* wherein ' His Goſpel has given it unto us, without Humane ' *Additions* & *Inventions*. Tis true, We have cauſe alwayes to blame our ſelves for our own *Deficiencies* in ſuch a Work of God. And if we give an Account of what we have done, it muſt be with an Holy Shame that we have *done ſo little*. *Pride*, and, *Vain-glorious Oſtentation*, Be thou at all poſſible Diſtance from the *Relation*, which our concern to have the Grace of God acknowledged, and a well-Deſigning Society of Good Men defended from Injurious Imputations, has compelled us to communicate unto the World.

It ſhall be done with all the *Modeſty* and *Brevity* that the matter will allow of.

In the Book Entituled, *Magnalia Chriſti Americana*, or, **The Hiſtory of** NEW-ENGLAND, there is a large
Account

Account of what was *formerly done*, for the Christiani-
zing of our *Indians*. Thither we refer the Reader, for
all that was *formerly done* : which when he Reads, he
will certainly wish for more ELIOT's in the World.
The present State of Christianity among them, is what
must now be Reported.

The Number of *Indians* in this Land, is not compa-
rable to what it was, in the middle of the former Century. The Wars which after an Offered and Rejected
Gospel, they perfidiously began upon the English, a-
bove Thirty years ago, brought a Quick Desolation
upon whole Nations of them. All that remain under
the English Influences in the *Massachuset*-Province, are
generally recovered out of their Paganism, to some
sense of the *Christian Religion.*

The Christianized Indians on the two Islands of
Martha's Vinyard, and *Nantucket* make a very considerable Body. At *Martha's* Vinyard and *Elsabeth's*
Islands, there are Ten Congregations, in which a glorious CHRIST is worshipped. There are Two Eng-
lishmen, and Ten Indians, that are Preachers to them,
in their own Language. They have *Schools* also, in
which their Children are taught to Read and Write;
and know the Catechism. At *Nantucket*, there are at
least Three Congregations; and more than as many
Preachers.

From these *Islands* we will pass to the adjacent *Con-
tinent*, Where a careful Enquiry has been lately made,
in a *Visitation* ordered for that purpose by the Com-
missioners for such affairs. The Result of the Enquiry was, That there are between Twenty & Thirty
Congregations of *Christianized Indians*, here on the
Main ; whereto there belong near Three Thousand
Souls. Here are Ten English Preachers, who give
them their Instructions and Assistences, and Preach unto them, either on the *Lords dayes*, or in appointed

Lectures

Lectures. There are also between Twenty & Thirty *Indian* Teachers, by whom the Exercises of the *Lords-dayes* are mostly managed. They have in several of these Villages on the *Main,* also made handsome Subscriptions of their own, towards the Building of *Meeting-Houses* ; wherein the English likewise have helped them. They have the whole *Bible* in their own Language ; which has been here twice Printed for them. This *Great Light* has been *Satellited,* with other Books which we have also Printed for them, in their own Language. Their Library is continually growing, by *New Books,* wherewith we Serve and Suit the Interests of Christianity among them, from time to time, as we see occasion. And their *Schools* are multiplying. *Family-Prayer* also is frequently upheld among them. And their *Marriages* are usually celebrated according to the Directions left by the famous ELIOT, whose Name still is of much Authority with them.

There are some Congregations of *Indians,* which are not advanced unto all the Priviledges of the *Evangelical Church-State* ; not yet combining for, and Enjoying of, all *Special Ordinances.* Yet a considerable Number of them are so ; and some *New Churches* have been lately form'd and fill'd among them.

The performances in the ordinary Congregations of the *Indians,* have been often such, that there are very many English Witnesses, who have not a little admired at the Gravity, the Attention, the Affection expressed in them. The pertinent *Prayers* (and, *Sine Monitore, quia de Pectore,*) the Orthodox *Sermons,* (at the Hearing whereof, the very Children of a dozen years old will readily turn to the Proofs,) and the Singing of *Psalms,* with a Melody out-doing many of the English, in their Meetings, have been frequently observed with Admiration. To see such forlorn Salvages, and the most ruteful Ruines of Mankind, not only *Cicurated*

into

into fome Civility, but alfo *Elevated* unto fo much
Knowledge and Practice of *Chriftianity*, has to fome
appeared an amiable and admirable Spectacle!

In their Churches, they have *Paftors* and *Elders* of
their own ; *Ordained*, Sometimes by the Hands of
Englifh Minifters ; and fometimes by the Hands of
the *Indian* Minifters, in the Prefence of the Englifh ;
All after the Solemn Englifh manner. And by *Admonitions* and *Excommunications* Publickly difpenfed,
they proceed againft Scandalous Offendors : for which
Intent, and that they may feafonably Find and Heal
all *Scandals*, they hold a *Church-Meeting* the Week before every Communion.

One that is at this Time, a Pious and Faithful Englifh Minifter, but Preaching alfo to the *Indians*, has
given in unto us, this Teftimony.

' Their Gravity, and diligent Attendence in
' the Time of Worfhip, with the affectionate
' Confeffions of fuch as are Admitted, into the
' Church, make me hope, that many of them may
' have the Work of the Spirit wrought in them,
' *according to the working of the mighty Power of God.*
' Their Method, refpecting thofe that are Admit-
' ted into their Communion, is more according to
' the manner of the Churches in the Primitive
' Times, than is now practifed among the Chur-
' ches in moft Parts. The Perfon to be Admit-
' ted, ftands forth in the midft of the Affembly ;
' and firft makes a *Declaration* of his *Knowledge,* and
' fometimes defires *Information* in things more ar-
' duous and doubtful. And then, he makes a
' *Confeffion of Sin* ; which they do, (as I have
' feen) with *Tears* and *Trembling,* like him in the

N 4 ' *Sixteenth*

‘ *Sixteenth* Chapter of the *Acts.* And then he
‘ gives an Account of *Experiences* he has had, of
‘ Convictions, Awakenings, and Comforts ; in
‘ which they are large and particular. After
‘ which (much Counsel and Exhortation,to re-
‘ main stedfast in the *Faith* and *Wayes* of the Lord,
‘ being given them, by their *Pastor* and *Elder*)
‘ they are Admitted. I would, (and not un-
‘ groundedly) hope, That *Additions* are *made*
‘ *unto the Church daily of such as shall be Saved.*
‘ There are many, which maintain a Christian
‘ Conversation, and are to be accounted, not
‘ *Almost,* but *Altogether Christians.* And this does
‘ Encourage the Preaching of the *Gospel* to them ;
‘ when we see, it pleases God to make it, *His*
‘ *Power unto Salvation.*

At present, we can do nothing for those Bloody
Salvages in the *Eastern Parts,* who have been taught
by the *French Priests,* That the Virgin *Mary* was a
French Lady, and that our Great Saviour was a *French-
man,* and that the *English* Murdered Him. and that He
Rose from the Dead, & is taken up to the Heavens, but
that all that would recommend themselves to His Favour, must Revenge His Quarrel on the English People; which issuing out from their Indiscoverable
Swamps, they have often done with cruel Depredati-
ons. When we have had the short Respites of a
Truce with them, we have made several New Attempts to carry them the Tenders of a *Glorious Gospel* ;
but they have presently broke out into Fresh Hostilities,
which have put an End unto all Good Expectations
concerning them.

There has been *Something done* to *Christianize* the
Mohegins, and other Indians, in the Colony of *Con-
necticut;*

necticut ; but, *Lord, who has believed* ! They have been obſtinate in their Paganiſm ; however their obſtinacy has not put an End unto our Endeavours.

An Exemplary Indian Miniſter, whoſe Name is *Japhet*, has of late years made ſeveral Salleyes, among his Pagan Country-men, about the *Narraganſet*-Country ; and the *Hand of the Lord has been with him*, and many *have Believed, and turned unto the Lord.*

We have made many Trials, to make the *Joyful Sound* of the Goſpel, reach unto the Five Nations, that are ſome Hundreds of Miles diſtant from us, to the Weſtward. All that is yet accompliſhed, is, To Support and Reward the pains of ſeveral *Dutch* Miniſters, who proceed as far as they well can, that theſe may no longer be ſuch *Fooliſh Nations* ; and have ſeen ſome comfortable Succeſſes of their Miniſtry.

The Principal concern for the Indians in the *Maſſachuſet*-Province, is to Preſerve and Improve the *Chriſtianity* already Profeſſed among them, and Prevent the loſs of a *Noble Work* by ſome Degeneracies, which have no very well boding Aſpect upon it : Eſpecially, to Prevent the Fatal Effects, with which the *Bottel* threatens it. In order hereto, various Methods are uſed continually, to keep a Watchful Inſpection on their Manners, and to make what Progreſs we can in *Anglicising* of them. Theſe things are in the *Practice* Encumbred with Difficulties, beyond what can be by moſt men in the bare *Theory* imagined. But the *Commiſſioners* here Entruſted, for the management of that Affayr, continually Conſult and Purſue, what may be moſt Subſervient unto the Grand Intention.

Adver-

ADVERTISEMENT.

IT is a Paſſage of the Incomparable BOYL;
' When I conſider, how much more to the
' Advantage of the Sacred Writings, and of
' Chriſtian Theology in general, diverſe Texts
' have been Explain'd and Diſcours'd of, by the
' Excellent *Grotius, Maſius, Mede,* and Sir *Francis*
' *Bacon,* and ſome other Late Great Wits, (to
' name now no Living ones,) in their ſeveral
' kinds, than the ſame Places have been hand-
'led by Vulgar Expoſitors, and other Divines ;
' And when I conſider, that none of theſe Wor-
' thies was at once a great Philoſopher and a
' Great Critick ; I cannot but hope, that when
' it ſhall pleaſe God, to ſtir up Perſons of a Phi-
' loſophical Genius, well furniſhed with Criti-
' cal Learning, and the Principles of true Phi-
' loſophy, and ſhall give them an Hearty con-
' cern for the Advance of His Truths, theſe men
' will make Explications, & Diſcoveries that ſhall
' be admirable. --- You ſhould no more meaſure
' the Wiſdom of God couched in the Bible, by
' the Gloſſes and Syſtems of Common Expoſitors
' and Preachers, than Eſtimate the Wiſdom He
' has Expreſs'd in the contrivance of the World,
' by *Magirus*'s or *Euſtachius*'s Phyſicks.

Many

Many years after this, the admirable *Witfius*
comforts us with a Paſſage of an obſervable Aſpect
that way ; ' *Neque profeƈto officio hic ſuo defuerunt*
' *Illuſtres Animæ.---*There have not been wanting
' thoſe Illuſtrious Men, who have obſerved all
' the Solid Diſcoveries in *Philoſophy,* all the curi-
' ous Reſearches of *Antiquity,* or that has occured
' in *Phyſick* or in *Law,* relating to the *Sacred*
' *Scriptures,* and have applyed it all with a Signal
' Dexterity to the *Illuſtration* thereof; And ſo 'tis
' come to paſs, that *Theology,* which had vaſt
' Riches of its own before, is now alſo Enriched
' with foreign *Spoiles,* and appears with thoſe
' Ornaments, which Extort, even from them that
' are moſt of all diſaffected unto it, a confeſſion
' of its moſt charming Majeſty.

The Noble Service to Mankind, thus propounded, having been ſo far Purſued, it is eaſy
to imagine, that a Perſon of but common Abilities, applying himſelf unto it, might accompliſh
a very *Rich Collection of Illuſtrations,* upon the glorious *Book of Truth and of Life.* It may not be a-
miſs, but the Treatiſe now in our Hands may
very agreeably do it, that the Friends of Learning and Religion be now 𝕬𝖇𝖛𝖊𝖗𝖙𝖎𝖋𝖊𝖉, of a
Moderate Performance, which by the Help of
Heaven, has been produced, of ſuch a Tendency.

No little part of what has been Written on the
Great Intention of *Illuſtrating the Divine Oracles,*
has been peruſed. Some Hundreds of the *Lateſt,*
as well as of the *Oldeſt* Writers, that have had any
thing

thing Looking that way, have been consulted. Many Thousands of their *Finest Thoughts* have been found out, Extracted, & Digested. The *Eye* of the Authors Industry, has not yet *Seen every Precious Thing* ; yet it has often, in the three Lustres of years, which have ran since he began his Undertaking, *Visited the Place of Sapphires*, and *found the Dust of Gold*, which is here Exposed unto the Refined part of Mankind, when it shall see cause to accept thereof. And there are Two Competent Volumns of the choicest 𝕴𝖑𝖑𝖚𝖘𝖙𝖗𝖆= 𝖙𝖎𝖔𝖓𝖘, (in *folio*) now lying ready for Publication.

The Work interferes not at all, with the Two very valuable Volumns of the POLAN *Annotations* ; but may ask for it, as an agreeable Honour, to attend upon them.

It is hoped, That all Impartial Christians, of whatever Denomination or Subdivision in Christianity, will esteem it, *An useful Work* ; For it must needs be so, if the Books, from which the *Best Things* are fetch'd, and laid here together, were so.

To bestow the censure of *Pride* and *Vanity*, on the Proposing of such a Work for Publication, would be there-with to Reproach all Attempts in such a way to Serve the Publick. 'Tis no Trespass against the Rules of *Modesty*, (but it would look like one against the Rules of *Equity* to call it so,) to give the Publick, a Report, and a Tender, of what has been thus Prepared. It is

is a *Lawful* and a *Modeſt* thing, for a Man to
Deſire, that ſo much of a Short Life, as has been
Spent in ſuch a Preparation, ſhould not be *Spent
in vain.*

The Author Lives in Daily Expeƈtation of his
Death ; But he Dies with ſome Hope, that the
Glorious Head of the Church, will ſtir up ſome
generous Minds, to forward an Undertaking So
Confeſſedly Worthy to be Proſecuted.

It is fit, that they ſhould be informed, Where
theſe Volumns ly waiting to be called for.
They are in a *Library*, to be ſoon found in the
American BOSTON. And this is the *Title* of them.

'BIBLIA AMERICANA. The Sa-
'cred Scriptures of the Old and New
'Teſtament. Exhibited, in the Order of Time,
'wherein the ſeveral and ſucceſſive Occurrences
'may direƈt the Placing and Reading of them :
'(which Exhibition alone, will do the Service
'of a Valuable Commentary.) With,

I. 'The common *Tranſlation*, with all due
'Modeſty, Amended and Refined in thoſe many
'Inſtances, where an Army of Learned and
'Pious Men in our Dayes, have with great *Rea-
·ſon*, Propoſed it.

II. 'A Rich Colleƈtion of *Antiquities* which
'the Studious Reſearches of Inquiſitive, and Ju-
'dicious Men in the Latter Ages, have recover-
'ed ; for a Sweet Refleƈtion of *Light* upon the
'Heavenly *Oracles* : In Multitudes of Paſſages ;
'and

‘ and particularly in thofe where the *Idolatry*, the
‘ *Agriculture*, the *Architecture*, and the Art of *War*,
‘ of the Former Ages is referr'd unto.

III. ‘ The *Types* of the *Bible* accommodated with
‘ their *Antitypes* ; And the *Bleſſed Book* yielding a
‘ vaſt mixture of Holy *Profit* and *Pleaſure*, even in
‘ thoſe Paragraphs of it, which have ſometimes
‘ appeared the leaſt Fruitful with *Inſtruction*.

IV. ‘ The *Laws* of the *Iſraelitiſh Nation*, in theſe
‘ *Pandects of Heaven*, interpreted ; and the *Origi-*
‘ *nal* and *Intention* thereof refcued from the Miſin-
‘ terpretations, that ſome famous Writers have
‘ put upon them. With a particular Hiſtory of
‘ the City *Jeruſalem*, under its wondrous Viciſſi-
‘ tudes, from the Dayes of *Melchizedeck*, down
‘ to ours ; and an Account of the preſent and
‘ wretched Condition, in which it waits the *Time*
‘ *to favour, the ſet Time to come on.*

V. ‘ *Golden Treaſures* fetch'd out of thoſe moſt
‘ *Unlikely Helps*, the *Talmuds*, and other *Jewiſh*
‘ *Writers* ; not only to Illuſtrate the *Oracles* once
‘ *Committed unto the Diſtinguiſhed Nation*, but alſo
‘ to Demonſtrate the Truth of *Chriſtianity*.

VI. ‘ *Natural Philoſophy* call'd in, to Serve *Scrip-*
‘ *tural Religion.* The faireſt *Hypotheſes* of thoſe
‘ *Grand Revolutions*, the *Making*, and the *Drowning*,
‘ and the *Burning* of the *World*, Offered. The
‘ *Plants*, the *Minerals*, the *Meteors*, the *Animals*, the
‘ *Diſeaſes*, the *Aſtronomical* Affairs, and the *Powers*
‘ of the *Inviſible World*, mention'd in the *Book* of
‘ GOD, repreſented with the *Beſt Thoughts of our*
‘ *Times* upon them. *VII.*

VII. ' The *Chronology* of this admirable *Book,* e-
' very where cleared from all its Difficulties; and
' the *Clock* of Time set Right in its whole Motion,
' from the Beginning of it.

VIII. ' The *Geography* of it *Survey'd* ; The Sci-
' tuation, especially of *Paradise* and of *Palestine,*
' laid out ; An Account given, how the whole
' Earth has been Peopled ; And many Notable
' and Enlightning Things contributed unto this
' Work by *Travellers,* of Unspotted Veracity.

IX. ' A sort of *Twenty-ninth Chapter* of the Acts ;
' Or, An Elaborate & Entertaining History, of what
' has befallen the *Israelitish Nation,* in every Place,
' from the Birth of the Glorious REDEEMER,
' to 𝔱𝔥𝔦𝔰 𝔳𝔢𝔯𝔶 𝔇𝔞𝔶 : And the present Con-
' dition of that Nation, the Reliques of the *Ten,*
' as well as of the *Two Tribes,* and of their anci-
' ent *Sects,* yet (several of them) Existing also,
' in the several Parts of the World, where they
' are now dispersed, at *this Time,* when their spee-
' dy Recovery from their Sad and Long Disper-
' sion is hoped for.

X. ' All *Appearance of Contradiction,* in the Pages
' fill'd from Inspiration, for ever taken away.

XI. ' The *Histories* of all Ages, brought in, to
' show how the *Prophecies* of this Invaluable *Book,*
' have had their most punctual *Accomplishment* ;
' and Strongly Established *Conjectures* on such as
' yet *remain to be Accomplished.* The most Unex-
' ceptionable Thoughts of the Ablest Writers on
' the *Revelation.* And the true Doctrine of the
' *Chiliad,*

' *Chiliad,* brought in, as a *Key,* to very much of
' the Wealth which the Church of God Enjoyes
' in this *Book* of the *Kingdom.*

　　XII. ' Some *Essayes* to Illustrate the *Scriptures,*
' from *Experimental Piety,* or the Observations of
' *Christian Experience.* And many of the *Excellent*
' *Things,* Observed in and Extracted from the
' *Holy Scriptures that make Wise unto Salvation,* by
' the *North-British Expositors,* who with a Pene-
' trating and peculiar Search after *Hints for*
' *Christian Practice,* have *Opened* many *Books* of
' the Bible.

　　' And many Thousands of Curious Notes,
' found Scattered and Shining, in the Writings
' both of the *Ancients* and the *Moderns,* laid here
' together in a grateful Amasment.

　　' All done with a strict adherence to the *Prin-*
' *ciples of Religion,* Professed in the most *Reformed*
' *Churches.*

　　' By the Blessing of CHRIST on the Labours
' of an *American.*

' 𝔍𝔫 𝔗𝔴𝔬 𝔄𝔬𝔩𝔲𝔪𝔫𝔰.

F I N I S.